Writing Readable Research

Equinox Textbooks and Surveys in Linguistics
Series Editor: Robin Fawcett, Cardiff University

Published titles in the series:

Analysing Casual Conversation
Suzanne Eggins & Diana Slade

Multimodal Transcription and Text Analysis
Anthony Baldry & Paul J. Thibault

Meaning-Centered Grammar
An Introductory Text
Craig Hancock

Genre Relations
Mapping Culture
J. R. Martin and David Rose

Language in Psychiatry
A Handbook of Clinical Practice
Jonathan Fine

The Power of Language
How Discourse Influences Society
Lynne Young and Brigid Fitzgerald

An Introduction to English Sentence Structure
Clauses, Markers, Missing Elements
Jon Jonz

Forthcoming:

Intonation in the Grammar of English
M. A. K. Halliday & William S. Greaves

Text Linguistics
The How and Why of Meaning
Jonathan Webster

The Western Classical Tradition in Linguistics
Keith Allan

Teaching Multimodal Literacy in English as a Foreign Language
Len Unsworth, Viviane Heberle and Robyn Louise Bush

Learning to Write/Reading to Learn
Scaffolding Democracy in Literacy Classrooms
J. R. Martin and David Rose

Multimodal Corpus-Based Approaches to Website Analysis
Anthony Baldry and Kay O'Halloran

Writing Readable Research

A Guide for Students of Social Science

by

Beverly A. Lewin

LONDON   OAKVILLE

Published by

UK: 1 Chelsea Manor Studios, Flood Street, London SW3 5SR
USA: DBBC, 28 Main Street, Oakville, CT 06779

www.equinoxpub.com

First published 2010

British Library Cataloguing-in-Publication Data

A catalogue record for this book is available from the British Library.

ISBN-13   978 1 904768 55 5   (hardback)
          978 1 904768 56 2   (paperback)

Library of Congress Cataloging-in-Publication Data
     Lewin, Beverly A, 1937-
      Writing readable research : a guide for students of social science /
     Beverly A. Lewin.
         p. cm. -- (Equinox textbooks and surveys in linguistics)
      Includes bibliographical references and index.
      ISBN 1-904768-55-5 (hb) -- ISBN 1-904768-56-3 (pb) 1. Social
     sciences--Authorship. 2. Communication in the social sciences. I.
     Title. II. Series.

      H61.8.L49 2006
      808'.0663--dc22

     2006010645

Typeset by Techastra, Hyderabad & Catchline, Milton Keynes (www.catchline.com)

Printed and bound in Great Britain

Table of Contents

Chapter 3: Using Verbs

Chapter 4: Shaping Sentences and Paragraphs

Chapter 5: Being Concise

Chapter 6: Making Connections—Connectives

Chapter 10: Results

Chapter 11: Discussion Sections

Chapter 12: Conference Texts

Chapter 13: Abstracts

Chapter 14: Writing Professional Letters

References

Preface

This book evolved from the materials I've developed over the years because I could not find a satisfactory textbook. They are either so general that they do not recognize the variations among fields or they are so specific that they focus on only one genre, such as experimental articles. Similarly, while some books concentrate on very specific local issues, such as punctuation and the use of the in/definite article, others give very general suggestions but no help in implementing them, e.g., *Write clearly, concisely and correctly* when novices have no idea of what 'concisely' means, to say nothing of 'clearly'. (In this book, Chapter 4, for instance, would aid in the implementation of 'concisely' while 'clearly' should be the result of implementing guidelines in several chapters.) No book can be everything to everyone, so I have striven for a middle approach.

For non-native speakers of English

I have paid special attention to the needs of those for whom English is a foreign language, by including special material on grammar, in Chapters 2 and 3, and by trying to write simply. However, the other chapters are relevant to any new writers, including native speakers of English.

For English speakers who are new to professional writing

The intended users of this textbook are novice writers, whether graduate students or new instructors. On the other hand, they are sophisticated scientists and therefore, I have tried to include rationale and historical background for some of the guidelines I give. In addition, new professionals need to understand some of the genres they will be faced with: journal articles, (Chapters 7–11), conference texts, (Chapter 12), abstracts (Chapter 13) and professional letters (14).

For social science students

Much of this book is devoted to general writing problems, in any field (Chapters 1–6; 12–14). However, this book is primarily intended for students of social science, which I define as fields that investigate human behavior. I relied on examples from anthropology, psychology, sociology, and communications. I have come to the conclusion that there is no such thing as 'scientific writing' or even 'social science writing'. Each discipline and type of research (e.g., theoretical vs. empirical models) has its own structure and language. For example, all social sciences do not share the same Introduction-Method-

Results-Discussion division and in fact, economics papers are more similar to mathematics papers than to sociology papers. Instead, I show how to analyze the structure in the reader's field.

Some textbooks present 'made up' examples; my students have argued that such examples are misleading and irrelevant. Hence, I have mostly relied on authentic examples; where there is no citation, the example is a paraphrase of texts I have read.

I have also tried to make the book stand on its own but ideally, it should be used as a course book, accompanied by class discussions on relevant points and a course instructor or other expert available to offer feedback on the tasks. I welcome input from readers. Suggestions should be sent to: lewinb@hotmail.com

Definitions

This is not meant to be a linguistics book. I have tried to keep explanations to a minimum and to state rules in very general terms. This aim means omitting all the deviations and irregularities that English is subject to. I have tried to concentrate only on what a person needs to know in order to produce a scientific text. Even so, Chapter 3, on Verbs is the longest in the book.

In order to use this book you do have to understand a minimal number of linguistic concepts, below:

text

This word is not meant to denote 'textbook'. It is an easy way to refer to any piece of discourse, whether partial or complete, spoken or written. It's easier than saying 'this article', 'this sentence' or 'this book'.

audience

Although this literally means 'listeners', we use it also to refer to readers of a specific text.

speaker

This term refers to the person delivering the message, whether orally or in writing. Similarly, the *receiver* of the message could be a listener or a reader.

clause

A clause is a group of words that includes a subject and a verb. One sentence can have more than one clause, as these 3 sentences do. I avoid using the term *clause* where possible because it sounds too technical but it is necessary when referring to components of a sentence. (Here is the last sentence divided into clauses: I avoid using the term *clause* where possible/because it sounds too technical/but it is necessary when referring to components of a sentence.)

Acknowledgements

This book is the result of 25 years of teaching and studying scientific writing and reflects insight from many people. First of all, I'd like to thank those who helped directly: Amy Kohn for her patient formating of a mass of words and Denis Shifrin for the illustration for 'passive' in Chapter 3.

Then, I'd like to thank my family—Larry, Alisa, Ilana, and Josh—for consultations and opinions on science and second language learning. I also appreciate their encouragement and patience while I've been preoccupied with this project. My lovely grandchildren contributed absolutely nothing to this book but they infuse me with love and joy, which keeps me going.

Lastly, I'd like to quote the literature. As Hanina the Sage (2000 B.C.E) said, I've learned much from my teachers, more from my colleagues, and most of all, from my students. This is my way of telling my students how much I gained from our joint work over the years.

Beverly A. Lewin

Chapter 1

What Are the Constraints in Scientific Writing?

When I meet my classes for the first time, I explain that scientific writing is very 'bounded' (constrained) by layers of rules and conventions that must be observed in order for the text to be publishable. Some students are very disappointed to learn that they are not free to express themselves or be 'artistic' or 'creative'. Similarly, this book is not a manual for 'creative writing'. You are entering a discourse community that defines what and how things should be said. However, we notice that some texts are more interesting, easier to read, even more dynamic than others. So even within the constraints, to some extent, an author can express his or her individuality.

What are the constraints in scientific writing in English that we have to master in order to succeed? Actually, the constraints divide into three areas: rules imposed by the English language on any discourse, whether written or spoken; accepted practices of writing on any subject; and conventions of scientific texts in particular. Perhaps we can say these constraints can be translated into four questions: Is the text phrased in 'good' English? Is the writing easy to read and interesting? Is it organized and argued according to the 'rules' of scientific articles? Has the author observed basic social conventions? I have broken down these aspects into the following categories, and I'm sure more can be added.

Grammar and Syntax

The grammatical and syntactic rules apply to anything that is written or said in English. These rules cannot be violated in academic writing. Just to give one example, the second sentence below violates a basic rule. (The asterisk [*] signifies that the sentence is ungrammatical.)

- The computer is a wonderful invention. *He can do many things.

The error is to use *he* to refer to a computer. In English, unlike many other languages, only human beings are classified into 'feminine' and 'masculine'. Everything else, such as a *chair* or *dependent variable*, is neuter and is referred to as *it* (singular) or *they* (plural). For guidelines for using acceptable English, see Chapter 2, Nouns and Pronouns; Chapter 3, Using Verbs; and Chapter 4, Shaping Sentences.

Register

This term refers to the choice of the appropriate words and grammar for the context. A major influence on that choice, in any communication, is sensitivity to the audience. For instance, compare these two letters requesting help:

a. Dear Professor X:
    I was wondering if you would be kind enough to give me your opinion on the following …

b. Dear Joe:
    Hi! Can you help me out? Please read the enclosed and send me feedback ASAP.

The choices for scientific texts are further refined by the 'academic' register and the sub-register for particular types of text (genres, below). The sentence * '*He can do many things*' in the above section, can be made grammatical as 'It can do many things' and might be found in a popular magazine. However, in a scientific paper, you would say 'The computer can perform many useful functions.' Similarly, scientists never *think, do, make or say* anything. Rather, they *propose* ideas, *perform* experiments, *construct* models, *claim* or *report* results. Occasionally, their results are *interesting* but never *exciting* or *terrific*.

Sometimes, scientists go overboard in translating ideas into scientific register. Consider the following three passages. Your job is to guess which one is *not* meant as a parody of academic writing.

1. (I have intentionally omitted this title.)

    Objective consideration of contemporary phenomena compels the conclusion that success or failure in competitive activities exhibits no tendency to be commensurate with innate capacity, but that a considerable element of the unpredictable must inevitably be taken into account. (Strunk & White, 1959: 17)

2. 'Dialectic desublimation and constructivist neocapitalist theory'

    If one examines textual desituationism, one is faced with a choice: either accept dialectic desublimation or conclude that the purpose of the participant is deconstruction, given that constructivist neocapitalist theory is invalid. Any number of discourses concerning Baudrillardist hyperreality may be found. (Scuglia & Hamburger, 2004: 1)

3. 'Ethical issues in the ethnography of cyberspace'

    For example, the increased importance of performance means there is a substantial potential for a substantive 'resocialing' of work

> in organizations, just as the decline of Modernism opens space for collective, situated ethics as opposed to individualized categorial imperatives. (Hakken, 2000: 170)

So which one is not a parody? Well, did you recognize (1) as George Orwell's 'translation' of a passage from the Bible (*Ecclesiastes*) into what we would call 'academic register'? The original English reads like this:

> I returned, and saw under the sun, that the race is not to the swift, nor the battle to the strong, neither yet bread to the wise …; but time and chance happeneth to them all.

And the second? It is completely meaningless and was randomly generated by a computer program called 'the Postmodern Generator'.

The third passage is not meant to be a parody, but it is so liberally sprinkled with 'buzzwords' that it seems like a parody. Even in context, it is difficult to understand.

The moral of the story is that you have to tune your text to the correct register but still find a happy medium between popular, informal language and overblown, esoteric, overly abstract jargon. I grant that you may find yourself swimming against the tide.

Style

In any field, or language, a text must be easy to understand and read. Sentences should not be too complex or too simple, heavy, or staccato. Redundant words dilute ideas. (See Chapter 5, Being Concise.) Repetitious sentence structure bores the reader. (See Chapter 4, Shaping Sentences, and Chapter 8, Review of Literature.) For instance, some reviews of literature look like this:

- Smith found X. Jones found Y. Cohen and Smith reported Z.

The sentences all follow the Subject–Verb–Object pattern. In addition, the author repeated *found* instead of using synonyms, which makes his prose grammatical but very monotonous.

Textual Cohesion

The reader looks for clear signals of organization in the text as a whole and between sentences and paragraphs. The sentences in the section above:

- Smith found X. Jones found Y. Cohen and Smith reported Z.

look like a supermarket list. There are no connections among these findings. (See Chapter 6 on Cohesion and Connectives.)

Cohesion also means that your reader can keep track of the people and places you've spoken about, and that your use of pronouns is consistent. (See Chapter 2, Nouns and Pronouns.)

Social Realities and Conventions

In addition to language constraints, a text must also reflect the given social 'rules' of the time and place in which it is written. Your audience will forgive you for breaking a grammatical rule but not for breaking a social rule, and possibly offending someone. To illustrate a simple 'social rule', let's look at the following quotation:

> Whenever a scientist communicates, even the most mundane and seemingly innocuous descriptions, he [sic] is persuading his audience, literally commanding them to adopt his point of view. (Weimar, 1977: 1)

When this text was published in 1977, it was acceptable to use masculine pronouns when referring to an unknown person, and maybe even most scientists *were* male. However, today one must acknowledge that a scientist or almost anyone else could be female and so we use *he or she* is persuading, *his or her* audience, and so on. If you notice, I added [sic] after the word *he* to indicate that was not my mistake but was in the original text. In general, for most publications in the social sciences, you now have to use the politically correct language stipulated in the style manuals of the American Psychological Association (2001) (APA), American Sociological Association (1997) (ASA) or in the particular style manual for your intended journal. These requirements ensure unbiased language when referring to both genders, all ethnic groups, and people with various physical attributes or sexual orientations.

When I use the words *politically correct*, I don't mean it sarcastically, although political correctness has been taken to extremes in some cases. I believe that being politically correct represents a modern understanding that words sometimes shape reality. Today's politically correct language is an attempt to get people to think differently about certain groups in society by changing their labels. For instance, if you speak about a *handicapped* person, it sounds as if the defect is in that person, not in an environment that is inhospitable to his or her difficulty. Would you say that someone like Stephen Hawking is handicapped? If you believe that words influence attitudes, you will welcome these changes, although there is a lot of work involved in using language that treats everyone with respect. (See Chapter 9, Methods.)

The sensitivity to the people you write about extends to the colleagues whose work you cite. What attitude towards fellow researchers is reflected in the following text?

> Jones and Smith (1993) built experimental systems which utilise the FM-SW technique. Their report did not suggest any solution to the mutual interference problem. Although Jones claimed to have one, they have not published it. [student text]

Although what she writes may be true, the author did not realize that her tone was rather accusatory. In addition to showing respect for your references, your writing also has to reflect sensitivity to your audience. Some variables to consider are: What is the power relation between you and your colleagues? Are they your students, peers or 'superiors' in the social hierarchy? Do you know them personally? Secondly, who are you? As a newcomer, you'll want to show a certain degree of modesty about your claims and not disparage other people's work but somehow push your own work forward in spite of these conventions. This topic is developed more fully in Chapters: 11, Discussions; 12, Conference Texts; and 14, Professional Letters.

Genre

An acceptable text not only observes the constraints listed above, but conforms to the pattern we expect for its category, or *genre*, be it newspaper editorial, recipe, or weather forecast. For instance, following are two texts; which one resembles the introduction to a research report in a scientific journal?

A. You're Wiser Now

> You react faster when you're young. There's no getting around it. But when people over 50 notice that they've lost a bit of that snap-crackle speed, they frequently overlook the mental powers they've gained in the bargain.

> 'In the old days, you called it wisdom,' says Duke University neurobiologist Lawrence Katz, Ph.D. 'But what is wisdom, really? It is a dense and rich network of associations developed through a lifetime of experiences.' ...

> Indeed, studies have shown that older adults are better at solving problems, more flexible in their strategies, and better able to keep their cool during a crisis than younger people are. They also tend to bounce back from a bad mood more quickly.

> Keep that in mind the next time you've wandering through a parking lot looking for your car. (Griffin, K., 2005: 51)

B. The Etiology and Treatment of Childhood

> [Sentences enclosed in square brackets are my additions]

> Childhood is a syndrome that has only recently begun to receive serious attention from clinicians. The syndrome itself, however, is not all that recent. ... The treatment of children, however, was unknown until this century, when so-called 'child psychologists' and 'child psychiatrists' became common. Despite this history of clinical neglect, it has been estimated that well over half of all Americans alive today have experienced childhood directly. (Seuss, 1983)

[Much interesting literature has been devoted to the clinical features of childhood (followed by literature review). However, no research has been devoted to treating this syndrome.]

'... the focus of this paper is on the efficacy of conventional treatment of childhood ...' .(adapted from Smoller, 1991: 207)

Even though the content is based upon scientific research, you can readily see that Text A is not a research report. Of course, the conversational register, such as *snap-crackle speed* identifies this as popular writing. But beyond that, it doesn't conform to the structure of a research article. There is no mention of what the purpose of the research is, for example. And a research article would never contain a personal suggestion such as in the last sentence.

In contrast, Text B sounds like a research report because it follows the expected structure, as well as register. However, it is based on nonsense. Incidentally, a lot of people get away with writing nonsense by adhering to the expected structure. In short, Text A is based upon scientific research but in the wrong structure, while Text B is based on a joke, 'dressed up' in the appropriate form or genre. For a fuller understanding of the concept of 'genre', see Chapter 7, Understanding genre analysis.

Medium

This constraint is imposed by the medium through which the text is transmitted, for instance, by speech or writing. If by speech, is it presented in the presence of the audience or via a telephone conversation? If by writing, is it transmitted by e-mail or by regular mail? Each medium engenders some new variations. The spoken style is very loosely packed, i.e., many words are used to give little information, while the written academic style is densely packed. Unfortunately, some professionals do not take medium into consideration. Thus, they read aloud a *written* text at a meeting. Similarly, sometimes students write a proposal as if they were speaking to colleagues in the same room. The new medium of e-mail combines features of both spoken and written texts; the jury is still 'out' in regard to which style should be followed. Of course, medium further restricts our register choices; for one thing, register can be more casual in spoken texts. Whereas, in a talk, you could say '*Finally, it's worth mentioning X*', in a formal paper you would say, '*It should be noted that ...*'

Field

A further constraint is imposed by the field we are writing about, e.g., chemistry or sociology. For example, in studying reviews of literature, Hyland

(1999) found that whether the name of the researcher is expressed (*Smith found*) or suppressed (*Smoking causes cancer[1]*) varies with field. The name of the researcher was expressed twice as frequently in citations in sociology as in physics. Similarly, I have noticed that chemists often completely obliterate the author by saying, *Ref. 17 found* ... a practice I have never seen in social science. Within the scientific community, each field has its own practices, including choice of verbs. (See Chapter 8, Review of Literature.)

Rhetoric

In the original sense, rhetoric means good writing. In Western tradition, all essays must have an introduction and a conclusion. Writing is divided into paragraphs and each paragraph is built around one main idea.

However, rhetoric in the popular mind refers to the art of persuasion. Unfortunately, it has a negative connotation, as when politicians use fallacious arguments to persuade the public. However, assuming our goals are innocuous, we needn't be ashamed that we are communicating to persuade the audience that our claims are valid and so on. In order to persuade you that there is a rhetorical aspect even to scientific writing, I am using the device of demonstrating support from another source:

> Whenever a scientist communicates, even the most mundane and seemingly innocuous descriptions, he [sic] is persuading his audience, literally commanding them to adopt his point of view. (Weimar, 1977: 1)

Whether you are conscious of it of not, rhetoric operates at every stage of writing, starting with the facts you select to be incorporated in the article. As Ralph Waldo Emerson put it:

- It is the fault of our rhetoric that we cannot strongly state one fact without seeming to belie some other. (Roberts, 2003)

Rhetoric also operates when you choose one word over another. For instance, animals are never *killed* after experiments are completed; they are *sacrificed* or *euthanized*, words which combine political correctness with making one's results more palatable.

Rhetoric operates at the sentence level, too, as in the following example. Suppose you have a choice between these two formulations of your results:

a. although these correlation coefficients were quite modest, they were all statistically significant. (Pennebaker & King, 1999: 1306)

b. although they were all statistically significant, these correlation coefficients were quite modest. [created example]

Which sentence is more persuasive? To answer that question, note that each sentence has two clauses, one beginning with 'although' and one beginning with a subject. The 'although' clause is a dependent clause; it cannot stand by itself. Now look at the main (independent) clause in each sentence:

a. [the correlation coefficients] were all statistically significant.

b. these correlation coefficients were quite modest.

Each sentence has a different emphasis.

Similarly, sometimes novice writers are too honest or present the 'negative' side of their findings instead of concentrating on the positive, as in:

- We were very surprised by the results; we expected the opposite to happen.

Attention to rhetoric would mean rephrasing this so that it does not leave the impression that the researchers were caught completely off guard.[1]

The rhetorical factor is most important in the Discussion section, in which one is actually building one's case for the validity and importance of the findings. See Chapter 11, on Discussions.

Where Do These Constraints Come From?

The origin of the social constraints is clear. As mentioned above, they are meant to keep the machinery of social relations well-lubricated. Many of the other constraints are biological in origin, that is, they are based upon the limitations of the human brain. For instance, short term memory can hold only a limited amount of information, so sentences should not be overladen with information nor should a verb be too far from its subject. Furthermore, it is easier to understand new information if it is formatted in a pattern (genre) we already know. But the evidence seems to show that some rules, like some grammatical rules, occurred spontaneously and quickly spread.

Putting It Together

In the above account, I've presented these constraints separately, as if they operate independently of one another. However, in reality, they overlap and interact. For example, a student wrote the following as the opening sentence to the introduction to his proposal:

- *I choosed this period because it seems to be a very important and unresearched one.

This sentence violates all the constraints simultaneously. For one, *choosed* is definitely ungrammatical and *unresearched* is questionable. Even if some people would accept it as grammatical, it isn't the usual word for the register. We can revise it to:

- I chose this period because it seems to be a very important and neglected one

but it still doesn't sound 'professional'. For one thing, the personal attribution (*I chose*) and the hedge (*it seems*) add extra words and weaken the statement rhetorically. Does this period just *seem* important? Why not state it unambiguously and more concisely, while using the opening sentence to give more information?

- XX is an important period because …. Yet little is known about it.

In addition, these two sentences now conform to the structure of the research report genre, as you will see in Chapter 7.

In conclusion, scientific writing goes through many filters before it sounds 'right'. The task sounds less formidable when we remember that in our other aspects of life, we have learned to navigate around all the constraints in the process of communicating ideas to other people.

Notes:

[1] To find out more about the difference between the actual events and feelings of the researchers and their eventual printed account, read Gilbert and Mulkay, (1984).

Chapter 2

Nouns and Pronouns

Introduction to Grammar

As scientists, you might find the 'rules' of grammar rather illogical. I have to agree with you. It would be better to think of these 'rules' as conventions that have evolved over time, rather than the product of a rational mind. Instead of trying to make 'sense' of them, keep in mind that language choices are culture bound; there is no reason that inanimate things should be classified as masculine or feminine, countable or uncountable, or *yin* or *yang*. These concepts do not correspond to 'reality'. They make sense only in the closed world of 'grammar'.

Nouns

We have to begin with defining the basic building blocks of a sentence. First, we'll define a **noun**, which is the name of anything: a **person** (*Charles Darwin*), a place (*South America*), or a **thing**, which can be abstract (*love*) or concrete (*table*). What is not so well known is that nouns also express a **quality** (*goodness*), an **idea** (*nationalism*) or an **activity**, as in '*Swimming* is good for you'.

Now, while Romance and many other languages divide things according to gender (masculine or feminine), English is a puritanical language that avoids sex. However, it applies another iron-clad distinction. What do you think is the grammatical distinction between the nouns in column A and those in column B, in Table 2-1?

Table 2-1   Types of Nouns

A	B
research	investigation
literature	article
advice	crisis analysis hypothesis basis axis

information	data
experience	equilibrium medium
equipment	kibbutz
damage	bushman
economics	syllabus
evidence	phenomenon criterion

The correct answer is that the nouns in column A are Uncountable, at least in English; there is no plural form. So you would say 'Economics **is** based largely on mathematics'. The count/uncount distinction is arbitrary. Other languages may consider research, for example, as a count noun, so that researches is acceptable in that language. To complicate matters, some nouns are flexible; we speak about 'the behavior of the children' in a general sense but psychologists do count behaviors as units in research. Similarly, we may speak of 'the damage done by the children' in a general sense, but lawyers speak of damages, meaning an amount of money paid to compensate an injured party. When you look up a noun in a good dictionary, the entry will say, 'N(oun), C(ount)' or 'N(oun), U(ncount)'. The word Uncount is used here instead of Non-count so that the abbreviation will not be NN.

Having crossed that barrier, and found that you have a countable noun, you must know how to form the plural. In column B, only investigation and article form the plural by adding s; all the other nouns have irregular plurals, which are usually signaled in the dictionary as pl. For some reason, many words have retained their Latin, Greek, or, in the case of kibbutz, Hebrew, plural endings.

I did include one tricky noun in column B—data is already plural. The singular, datum, is never used or at least, I've never seen it, probably because no one can publish a paper supported by only one datum. Therefore data takes the plural form of the verb: the data **are** interesting. I know that you will see aberrations such as researches and more often, data **is**, in the literature, but we have higher standards, don't we?

To save you the trouble of looking them up, the plural forms of all the nouns in column B are in Table 2-2:

Table 2-2   Plural Forms of Nouns

Singular	Plural
investigation article	regular: add s
crisis analysis hypothesis basis axis	crises analyses hypotheses bases axes
datum	data
equilibrium medium	equilibria media
kibbutz	kibbutzim
bushman	bushmen
syllabus	syllabi
phenomenon criterion	phenomena criteria

The count/uncount distinction involves other rules. As I said earlier, uncount nouns can only take the singular form of the verb. Similarly, certain quantities are expressed differently for count and uncount nouns, as in the following sentences.

Uncount:

> *Much* research *has* been done on the role of language but *little* research *has* shown the role of grammar in everyday life.

> *The amount* of research *is* very small.

Count:

> *Many* investigations of language acquisition *have* been done on four-year-old children but *few* investigations *have* involved two-year-olds.

> *The number* of investigations *is* very small.

Determiners

Count nouns have other peculiarities. A singular count noun can never be left 'bare' as in *Every night I read <u>book</u>. A singular count noun is (almost) always preceded by a 'handle', which can be an article - definite (*the*) or indefinite (*a*) - or another member of a class of items, called 'determiners'. Roughly put, determiners make the noun more specific, e.g., by *this, that, these, those, my, your, his, her, its, our, their* or by indicating the quantity of the noun: *a few, a little, both, much, several, twenty-five* and so on. The determiner can be followed by an adjective, e.g., *some* (det) *heavy* (adj) *books* (noun). (In contrast, Uncount nouns may be preceded by a determiner or left bare, e.g., I like coffee.) Table 2-3 shows examples of the use of articles.

Table 2-3   Definite vs. Indefinite Noun Phrases

	Definite	Indefinite
Singular	*The book* that I wanted	Every night I read *a book*.
Plural	*The books* that you ordered	*Books* are important for a child's education.

> ## Task A: Clothing bare nouns
>
> The underlined nouns in the following sentences have been left 'bare'; correct them so that they are either definite or indefinite and either singular or plural:
>
> First <u>question</u> deals with time <u>factor</u>.
>
> We will study individual <u>difference</u> in response to traumatic <u>event</u>.
>
> (There is more than one possibility for each answer. Answers are at the end of this section.)

The definite article *the* is one of the most complicated items to explain and I don't think any non-native speaker can learn all the rules. Besides, like countability in nouns, *the* is rather flexible. As you learned in school *the* is used to refer to something you've already mentioned, i.e., known to the audience, as in the second sentence:

- Someone gave *an* interesting *talk* [first mention = indefinite] at the conference.
- Unfortunately, *the talk* [now we know which talk you mean] was in French, so it was wasted on me.

But in academic writing, *the* can also be used even though you haven't mentioned a particular noun as in:

- Changes are taking place in *the family*

meaning all families, not a specific family you have mentioned, although:

- "Changes are taking place in *families*" is also acceptable.

Nouns are often accompanied by descriptive words, forming *a noun phrase*. Even at first mention, *the* is necessary when you are making your noun (phrase) very specific, as in:

- I will now explain *the* conceptual and practical reasons that underlie decisions.

☹ Watch out:

> When a plural noun is used to describe a noun immediately following, it changes to singular form and only the final noun takes the plural, so that *animals behavior* becomes *animal behavior*.

Task B: Noun phrases

Correct the following noun phrases: *drugs abuse, *a five-years-old boy, *females alcoholism. Answers are at the end of this chapter.

Pronouns

What Are Pronouns?

The following text illustrates what a world without pronouns would look like:

> **Vicarious Punishment in a Work Setting**
>
> After the supervisors completed the output check, **the supervisors** walked back to the confederate's table and administered the punishment. In two groups, the confederate was told that **the confederate's** output was significantly lower than **the confederate's** co-workers and that if **the confederate** did not increase **the output**, the supervisor would have to cut **the confederate's** pay. (Adapted from Schnake, 1986: 344)

This text is technically grammatical but very unnatural, boring, and perhaps confusing. You might not even realize that all the instances of *the confederate* refer to the same person. We have an easy solution. If the original noun (referent) is easy to remember (not more than a sentence away), we substitute a handy word, called a pronoun (meaning that it stands for a noun). Below is the original text:

> After the supervisors completed the output check, **they** walked back to the confederate's table and administered the punishment. In two groups, the confederate was told that **her** output was significantly lower than **her** co-workers and that if **she** did not increase **it**, the supervisor would have to cut **her** pay. (Schnake, 1986: 344)

So we have examples of a few pronouns in Table 2-4, to which I've added two (not in the original text), to make the list complete (Table 2-5).

Table 2-4   Illustrated Pronouns

Noun	Singular or Plural	Human/Non-Human	Pronoun
supervisors	plural	human	**they**
output	singular	non-human	**it**
the confederate	singular	human	**she** (female)
the confederate's	singular	human	**her** (female)

Table 2-5   Singular vs. Plural Pronouns

	Singular	Plural
Human	She (He) *The confederate*	They *supervisors*
Non-human	It *output*	They *(computers)*

The above examples all refer to concrete entities. What about abstract concepts? In the same article, the author gives the background for his study:

> … the use of punishment is a common occurrence in organizations, although organizational researchers have avoided **this** (1) area. **This** (2) is no doubt due to the widely held view that not only is punishment less effective than positive reinforcement but that **it** (3) also results in undesirable side effects. [N & N] (1980) point out, however, that **there** (4) is little empirical evidence for either of **these** (5) criticisms. (Schnake, 1986: 343)

1. The author uses a pronoun (**this**) and *area* instead of repeating *the use of punishment*.

2. **This** apparently refers to the claim that 'researchers have avoided this area'. (More about *this* later.)

3. Our common sense tells us that **it** refers to *punishment* and not to *positive reinforcement*, which is its nearest neighbor.

4. **there** is one of those empty pronouns; it has no referent but it makes it easier to start certain sentences, e.g.:

   - A penguin is sitting on the ice. = **There** is a penguin sitting on the ice.

The other pronoun that can be used without a referent is *it*, as in:

   - **It** is important/interesting/to remember X = X is important, interesting

5. *these criticisms*: *these* refers to nouns, plural. Instead of repeating the criticisms, the author just refers to them as *these criticisms*, i.e., the ones that have already been mentioned.

☹ Watch out: ***this*** *area* (singular). (Think of the 'i' as the number 1) but ***these*** *criticisms* (plural).

Table 2-6   Location determiners

Location: Physical & Abstract	Singular	Plural
Near	Read **this** book	Read **these** books
Far	Read **that** book	Read **those** books

Table 2-7   Pronouns for Different Functions

Subject poss.+noun	poss. – noun	object
I am reading **my** book.	This book is **mine**.	Give it to **me**.
We are reading **our** book.	This book is **ours**.	Give it to **us**.
You are reading **your** book.	This book is **yours**.	I'll give it to **you**.
He is reading **his** book.	This book is **his**.	Give it to **him**.
She is reading **her** book.	This book is **hers**.	Give it to **her**.
The book is good, but not **its** ending.	None!	I will write a new ending for **it**.
They are reading **their** book.	The book is **theirs**.	Give it to **them**.

When Do We Use Them?

It is generally preferable to use a pronoun instead of repeating a noun, especially, if the noun has a string of modifiers attached as in the subject of the following sentence:

The university cafeteria prices were too high; recently, **they** have been increased still further.

Don't use a pronoun when the meaning is ambiguous, i.e., when the pronoun could reasonably refer to more than one entity, as in:

• Mr. Brown and his father are both scientists but **he** is a biochemist.

Or more serious (or even fatal):

• The scientist wiped the smudges off the test tubes with her fingers, and put **them** into a sterilizer.

Various scenarios can be imagined, depending upon whether *them* refers to *smudges, test tubes,* or *fingers.*

But the one I like the best is this query to a newspaper columnist:

• My neighbor walks her dog in her dressing gown early in the morning. I think this is inappropriate. What do you think?

Columnist: If the dog is wearing the dressing gown, then this is certainly inappropriate. (Novis, 2002: 6)

Avoid a 'bare' **this** and **that** with no noun attached. In the passage below, the first **this** is joined to a noun, **area**, but the second **This** is bare:

- … the use of punishment is a common occurrence in organizations, although organizational researchers have avoided (1) **this** area. (2) **This** is no doubt due to

Try to make it clear to which words or parts of the sentence the pronoun refers. In the above case, it would have been preferable to say:

- **This avoidance** (or reluctance) is no doubt due to …

Make sure you are consistent throughout the passage, unlike, e.g., 'The company ought to treat **its** employees equally, both in allocating workers to jobs and in **their** reward system.' Both pronouns should be either **its** or **their**, but not one of each. Your choice depends upon whether you think of a company (or other group of people) as acting as single individuals or as one unit.

Whose

Whose is a totally misunderstood but very handy pronoun. Suppose you want to connect sentences such as these, using *the book* as the 'glue':

- I read a book about ecology. I can't remember the author of the book.

You could say, as we did in my day when everything was more difficult:

- I read that book, the author of *which* I can't remember.

However, these days you can just say:

- I read a book about ecology, *whose* author I can't remember.

☹ Watch out: *whose* (a possessive pronoun) is not *who's* (a contraction for *who is*) nor will it ever be!

Ideological and Political Issues

As I have said earlier, often ideology intersects with grammar.

We vs. I

The APA Manual (2001) advises against the use of *we* if you are the sole author of the paper.

He, She, or It

Secondly, in English, unlike many other languages, only human beings are classified into 'feminine' and 'masculine'. Everything else, such as a chair or a variable, is neuter and is referred to as **it** (singular) or **they** (plural). The only human who might properly be referred to as **it** is a baby as in: *The baby usually knows its mother by the age of 3 days.* (Animals are technically **it** or **they** if they are used in research. A household pet is another matter I won't get into.)

☹ Watch out: don't use **he** or **she** for an inanimate object; don't use **he** when it can refer to a male or a female.

He vs. She

Now we come to a really hot political issue. How are we going to refer to people? In my schooldays, back in the 1950's, you were expected to use the masculine pronoun when you meant a male or female, as in: '*The student should turn in his library books at the end of the semester.*' Now, in order to be egalitarian, we must say **his** or **her** library books (or even **her** or **his**). This system is fair but cumbersome. In order to be egalitarian in this book, I have tried to alternate between the feminine and masculine forms.

A third system is to use the plural form, even when a singular noun may seem more appropriate:

- **Students** must return **their** books …

Or omit the agent when appropriate:

- Books must be returned …

That vs. Who

Instead of worrying about the sex (gender) of inanimate objects, the English pronoun system is obsessed with whether the entity referred to is human or non-human. The following shows how this distinction comes into play when we use *relative pronouns*, those that join a subject to a description. The relative pronoun for a human being is *who*; the relative pronoun for non-humans is *that*:

1. **People who** live in glass houses shouldn't throw stones.

   The first person who was available was hired.

2. **The book that** I wanted was published in 1945.

(By the way, the pronoun **whom**, as in '*The person whom I saw yesterday*' was discarded even before **he** was abolished as the universal pronoun.)

Restrictive Pronouns: That vs. Which

Both *that* and *which* refer to non-human entities, but with an important difference:

> We will examine **two theories that** (1) can explain this phenomenon. According to **the first theory, which** (2) is accepted in the literature, the

increase in population is caused by a high birthrate. **The alternative theory, which** (3) will be presented in this paper, claims that the increase in population is caused by a low death rate. [created example]

Explanation:

1. **that** links **two theories** to the description **can explain this phenomenon.** *That* distinguishes them from other theories and tells you specifically which ones I mean.

2. **which** gives you additional information about this alternative theory, but it doesn't distinguish it from all other theories. Look at the difference:

   a. **the first theory, which** is accepted in the literature, … (doesn't tell me whether other theories are accepted)

      the first theory that is accepted in the literature, … (tells me that there are other theories that are also accepted)

   b. **The alternative theory, which** … (tells me there is only one alternative theory)

      The alternative theory that … (incorrectly tells me that there is more than one alternative theory)

Notice also that **which** is preceded by a comma but there is no comma before **that**. (See section on Punctuation, Chapter 4.)

Task C: Relative pronouns

Fill in the correct pronouns in the following passage.

Locusts, _____ were sent as a plague on the ancient Egyptians and _____ have reappeared in the Middle East over the millennia… do not arrive by chance along with prevailing winds.

This common wisdom has been overthrown by scientists at the Hebrew University of Jerusalem, _____ have shown that these overgrown flying grasshoppers have a physiological trait called polarization vision, _____ provides them with a built-in source of 'surface analysis.' (Siegel, 2005: 5)

Answers to Tasks

Task A: Clothing bare nouns

Possible answers to questions: (assuming there can be only one *first question*)

1. *The* first question deals with *the* time factor.

   The first question deals with time factors.

   The first question deals with *a* time factor.

2. We will study individual *differences* in response to traumatic *events*.

   We will study individual *differences* in response to *a* traumatic *event*.

   Not likely but possible:

   We will study *an* individual *difference* in response to *a* traumatic *event*.

   We will study *an* individual *difference* in response to traumatic *events*.

Task B: Noun phrases

Corrections for noun phrases: **drug** abuse, a five-**year**-old boy, **female** alcoholism.

Task C: Relative pronouns

The original article, undoubtedly written in a rush, contained two errors, which I have corrected below.

> Locusts, **which** were sent as a plague on the ancient Egyptians and **which** have reappeared in the Middle East over the millennia … do not arrive by chance along with prevailing winds.

> This common wisdom has been overthrown by scientists at the Hebrew University of Jerusalem, **who** have shown that these overgrown flying grasshoppers have a physiological trait called polarization vision, **which** provides them with a built-in source of 'surface analysis.' (Siegel, 2005: 5)

Chapter 3

Using Verbs

Information is expressed in clauses containing a subject (in the form of a **noun or pronoun**), discussed in Chapter 2, and a **verb**. **Verbs** tell you what the subject does, as in 'Smith *writes* books', or link the subject to a description, with a form of the verb *to be*, as in 'Smith *is* tired/in the next room/a colleague of Jones' or with another linking verb, such as 'Smith *became/seems/appears* unhappy'.

When using nouns, the writer has to decide if they are singular or plural. Verbs, however, are more complicated; the speaker has to choose the tense, the perspective (passive or active), and perhaps add comments, such as an estimation of the possibility of that action actually occurring, among other things. This chapter will deal with those choices.

As I said in regard to **nouns**, the rules of grammar are the products of conventions rather than of rational design. When you read about tenses, you will see that not all the meaning is expressed by the tense; the meaning of the statement depends upon many contextual cues that the audience interprets. For instance, if the speaker says *Smith has written many books*, the native speaker of English understands that Smith is probably still alive and still writing, while the sentence *Smith wrote many books* seems to 'close the book' eternally on Smith. To keep this text brief, I don't provide the appropriate context for sentences for my examples. In real life, you would have much more information from which to understand the message of the speaker.

Tenses In General

The main choice to make when using a verb in a sentence is its *tense*, the grammatical system we use to express *time*. *Time* and *tense* are not always the same. For instance, in English, future time can be expressed by the present tense:

- Tomorrow, I go to Paris

or the future tense: (strictly speaking, there is no future tense in English, as you need to add another verb, *will*, to form it)

- Tomorrow, I will go to Paris.

23

The divisions of time, like the division of nouns into count/uncount categories, are conventional; different cultures divide time differently. In Hebrew, the 'day' begins at sundown, whereas in English, it begins at 12 midnight. Similarly, the distinctions involved in *tenses* are culture-bound. While some languages distinguish only between a finished and an unfinished action, English distinguishes among the past, the present, and the future, and allows for different variations within those periods. Unfortunately, we will have to review these tenses, so please check what you already know, by choosing the appropriate phrase from group B to complete the following sentences. There should be only one appropriate phrase for each blank.

Task A: What Are the Tenses Used For?

Group A

1. The sun sets _____
   (present simple)

2. The sun is setting _____
   (present continuous)

3. The sun set _____
   (past simple)

4. The sun has set _____
   (present perfect)

5. The sun has been setting _____
   (present perfect continuous)

6. The sun was setting _____
   (past continuous)

7. The sun had set _____
   (past perfect)

Group B

now; already; yesterday at 7 p.m.; earlier and earlier; before he finished his work; when the accident occurred; in the west

---

Here is a brief explanation of each tense. In the next section, an explanation will be given of how they are used in scientific writing. I use the word 'tense' rather broadly. Actually, the continuous (–ing form) is not a tense but a variation of past or present.

1. **The sun sets in the west**.

   The verb in the present simple (*sets*) denotes a regular occurrence, or, as in this case, a natural phenomenon. Oddly, the present simple tense is not restricted to the present time; in this case, for example, it is always true or timeless.

2. **The sun is setting now**.

   The present continuous should only be used when the event is current. A good test is if you can properly add the word *now* to the sentence. The *now* can be literal, meaning 'at this instant', as in (2), or in a general sense, meaning 'nowadays', as is understood in 'Serious criminal behavior committed by female gang members ... *is becoming* more common'. (Molidor, 1996: 251)

3. **The sun set yesterday at 7 p.m.**

   The past simple (*set*) indicates something that was over in the past; that is, it is not true at the time of speaking. Compare to (4).

4. **The sun has set already**.

   The present perfect (*has set*) is the most difficult (or illogical) of all the tense variations. It is neither *present* nor *perfect* but denotes that the statement is 'true' as of the present and it is *perfect* in the sense of completed rather than faultless. In contrast to the past simple, this tense is often used to show that the action was completed recently (as in the above sentence) or is not necessarily over, such as:

   - I have taught English for five years.

   Most of all, it implies that the action had a beginning; it is not timeless. Refer to the **timeline**, below, to see how this tense is used in scientific articles.

5. **The sun has been setting earlier and earlier**.

   This is rather a silly sentence, because in winter, it would be obvious, but we can envision someone saying this in exasperation rather than in order to provide information. The present perfect continuous tells us that the action has been repeated, and can be expected to recur in the near future.

6. **The sun was setting when the accident occurred**.

   Remember learning in school about one short action occurring during a longer one, as in *The phone rang while I was taking a shower*? The past continuous is used <u>only as background</u> for another past action. It is rarely needed in social science; perhaps in a methods section, the authors might say something like:

   - For the experiment, we selected 104 participants, of whom, 50 people were working full time and 54 were working part-time....

Obviously here, the authors did interrupt these hapless people in the middle of their working life. The following sentence shows the past continuous used to denote two actions going on simultaneously:

- It was made clear to the participants that the discussions that they were attending was one of three sessions that we were evaluating.

7. **The sun had set before he finished his work.**
   In this case, one action (*the sun set*) occurred <u>before</u> another past action (*he finished his work*). The past perfect, like the past continuous, is used only in conjunction with another action. A historian might need to use this, as in:

   - Smith had consolidated his power before he was elected in 1933.

In this sentence, the time is clear because the writer uses *before*, but it is possible that the reader might have to depend on the tense to understand the sequence, as in:

- Smith was elected in 1933. He had consolidated his power by killing off the opposition.

In the following example, we are dependent upon the past perfect to understand the chronological order of the actions. First, the author describes the sample, e.g., *The sample size was 145*. Later, she tells us that:

- Most participants **had participated** in workshops to sensitize them to the experience of immigration. (Ben-David, 1996: 30)

We therefore understand that the workshops took place **before** the experiment.

To sum up, let's look at this Timeline of actions according to their point of completion:

The Past			Moment of Speaking
Completed before another past action	**Completed within a specific time frame**	**Recent Past (a) and possibly continuing (b)**	
The sun had set before he finished his work	The sun set yesterday at 7 p.m.	(a) The sun has set already -----> (b) I have lived here since 2005->	

Tenses in Social Science Writing

In General

If you're thinking that the tense system looks too complex, don't despair! Although I have included seven tense variations (above) in order to give the complete picture, only the first four are used in social science. The others almost never appear in scientific texts, whereas they are common in stories.

Look at the differences among the present tense variations; they all are grammatically correct, but they convey different messages, in parentheses.

1. **Unemployment leads to poverty...**
   (This fact is always true; we don't see a beginning or end to it.)

2. **Unemployment has led to poverty...**
   (This fact is true in a number of cases only or only recently)

3. **Unemployment is leading to poverty..../Unemployment has been leading to poverty**
   (This fact is true now, but maybe temporary; it doesn't tell us about the past)

The present continuous is rarely used and would be needed only in fields that deal with new, or transient phenomena, as in:

- Serious criminal behavior committed by female gang members ... *is becoming* more common. (Molidor, 1996: 251)

This doesn't mean that the choice of the tense is solely dependent on the message you want to convey. On the contrary, there are some grammatical constraints. An asterisk (*) indicates that the sentence is ungrammatical, as in the next two cases.

You **cannot** use the present perfect when you specify a period of time that is over as in:

- *In 1988,* Smith has reported ....

You **must** use the past simple in this case.

Conversely, you **can't** use the past simple when you specify a period of time that is *not* over as in:

- *Since 1988, /this year* researchers investigated the effects of ....

You **must** use the present perfect in this case. *Researchers have been investigating/have investigated the effects of ....*

On the other hand, you **can** choose the time period according to the type of statement you want to make, e.g., *Recently, Jones has found ....* or *Last week, Jones found ....*

Use the present simple **not the present continuous**:

1. to describe natural or social phenomena or generalizations
   - Praying for help and healing <u>is</u> a fundamental concept in practically all societies. (Byrd, 1988: 826)

2. to state facts about literature or your current paper

- Shakespeare <u>writes</u> about love; Table II <u>shows</u> the variation; in this paper, we <u>present</u> a new algorithm

3. to describe certain methods that are still current

- Usually, we <u>calculate</u> x by …

Use the present perfect:

1. to show an accumulation of actions until the present time:

- Many studies <u>have shown</u> …

2. to show recent, not timeless, phenomena. In some cases, we depend on the meaning of the verb, rather than the tense, to understand whether the action is complete:

- The play <u>has begun/ended</u>; AIDS <u>has become</u> widespread; a shift toward self – employment <u>has taken</u> place

Use the present perfect continuous to show an action that is continuing:

- For not only did the volume and rate of nonagricultural self-employment stabilize in the 1950's, they <u>have been declining</u> once again since 1983. (Linder & Houghton, 1990: 727)

Use the past simple when you want to convey that an event is **over/limited**.

- We thought that X = Y. (You could conceivably continue with "But now we think …")

or, as noted, if you situate the action in a period of time that is over as in:

- Last year, John's article appeared.

The following sets of sentences contrast some of the troublesome tenses. What is the difference in meaning between (a) and (b) in each group below?

1. My experiment shows that

   a. anxiety <u>prompts</u> smoking ….

   b. anxiety <u>prompted</u> smoking ….

2. a. Smith <u>wrote</u> many papers.

   b. Smith <u>has written</u> many papers.

3. a. When I arrived home, I saw that thieves <u>had been</u> in the house.

   b. When I arrived home, I saw that thieves <u>were</u> in the house

4. a. In 2004, it <u>was found</u> that ….

   b. In the past few years, it <u>has been found</u> that ….

5. a. They <u>have been working</u> on this problem for ten years/since 1998.

    b. They <u>worked</u> on this problem for ten years.

In (1a), the author makes her findings into a generalization, as if the question of what prompts smoking has now been solved. In (1b) the author restricts her claim to the findings in this particular experiment.

The sentences in (2) show us how much we can infer from the tense, independent of the meaning of the verb itself. In (2a), we infer that poor Smith will not be writing any more papers. In (2b), we infer that Smith is still hard at work.

In (3a), we can tell that, fortunately, the thieves had left before the speaker got there. But (3b) indicates that the speaker arrived home at the same time that the thieves were in the house.

Statement (4b) seems more recent and relevant to an English speaker than (4a) regardless of the actual lapse of time.

This is what you can infer from (5): In (a) they're still working, while in (b) they are not working on it now.

Tenses in Reviewing the Literature

Grammar is easy when you need to express only one action in each sentence. But when you get to the review of literature, you have two actions in one sentence, the first stating the research narrative and the second stating the conclusion about the phenomenon, as in:

- (1) Smith (1996) <u>reported</u> that (2) smoking <u>decreases</u> the desire for food.

These two actions occur at different times and in theory, at least, the decision for each is made independently on rhetorical grounds.

The possibilities for part (1), the research narrative, are: Smith (1996) **reports/ has reported/reported** that …, depending on the considerations discussed above. However, the APA style manual (2001) recommends that you use only the past simple (**reported**) or present perfect (**has reported**) for citing the literature. In addition, I notice that some verbs are used in only one tense, e.g., Smith **found** (never **finds**, or **has found**).

The possibilities for part (2), stating of the phenomenon, are:

- smoking **decreases** the desire for food (the finding is stated as a generalization, always true) or

- smoking **decreased** the desire for food (the finding is limited to this particular study)

The possible combinations are:

- **Smith (1996) reports** that smoking decreases the desire for food.
- **Smith (1996) reports** that smoking decreased the desire for food.
- **Smith (1996) reported** that smoking decreases the desire for food.
- **Smith (1996) reported** that smoking decreased the desire for food.
- **Smith (1996) has reported** that smoking decreases the desire for food.
- **Smith (1996) has reported** that smoking decreased the desire for food.

The last two sentences are grammatical but the present perfect is more usually used with a subject that indicates an accumulation of studies rather than one study, as in:

- **Many investigators have reported** that smoking decreased the desire for food.

Using the Tenses

After choosing the appropriate tense, the next question is how to change (conjugate) verbs to indicate the tense. Table 3-1 summarizes the basics. Chances are you will not use the future tense in a scientific text but you may for other professional purposes.

Table 3-1   Verb Tenses

Tense	Static	Continuous
Present		
Non-perfective	I <u>write</u> directly on the computer	I *am writing* to ask you ….
Perfective	I <u>have written</u> several letters to them	I *have been writing* all day and I'm tired.
Past		
Non-perfective	Yesterday, I <u>wrote</u> a book; what did you do?	While I *was writing*, my computer crashed.
Perfective	I decided to call him after I <u>had written</u> to him many times.	I *had been writing* to him for many years before I actually met him.
Future		
Non-perfective	I <u>will write</u> when I get there.	Don't bother me tonight; I *will be writing* a book.
Perfective	I <u>will have written</u> 10 letters by next Tuesday.	(Rare) By the time I retire, I *will have been writing* articles for 40 years.

To form the present perfect and past perfect, you need a structure called the *past participle*. You will find it in a verb table, a sample of which is illustrated below in Table 3-2. It presents the three basic forms of the verb: the base form, which is the infinitive without 'to', the past simple, and the past participle, which is the form you need for the past or present perfect and for the passive. Most verbs follow the regular pattern and you can find the irregular ones in the dictionary.

Table 3-2   Verb Forms

Type	Base	Past Simple	Past Participle (PP)
Regular	study	studied	studied
Irregular	write	wrote	written
	do	did	done

Conjugating the Verbs

Present Simple

The past tense is easy: *I wrote, she wrote, they wrote,* etc. But the tricky part is the present simple. While we say: *I/we write, you write, they write,* we have a slight variation when the subject is the 'third person' (the thing spoken about) (*the sun, society, research, Jones*), which you will be using most often. When the subject is plural, the verb is 'singular' and vice-versa. An easy way to remember this is to imagine you have one $ for every sentence in the present simple, when the subject is in the third person. You can either use the $ for the subject or the verb **but not both**, in contrast to many other languages, which use a plural verb with a plural subject. So you have:

- The author$ write ....

    or

- The author write$ ....

Of course, the rule applies to irregular plural forms, too, which don't take 's':

- These data (pl.) appear ....

And uncount nouns are always considered singular:

- The research shows ....

Present Perfect

The only part of the verb that changes according to the subject is *have* although the participle remains constant:

- I/we/you/they *have* written ...
- She/he/it *has* written ...

In the **past perfect**, there are no changes according to subject

- I/we/you/she/he/they *had* written …

In **Noun of Noun phrases** (such as *a basket of fruit*).

1. The **significance** of these symptoms **is** discussed below.
2. The **results** of the investigation **are** inconclusive.
3. A number of **people were** interviewed.

Interestingly, the verb agrees with the first noun in the subject in (1) and (2). But the verb agrees with the second noun in the subject in (3). This seems to follow common sense. What is 'discussed below' in (1) – the *significance* or the *symptoms*? What is inconclusive – the *results* or the *investigation*? Who was interviewed – *a number* or *people*?

The Passive

The passive form of verbs is not just a grammatical category; it is a highly charged political issue in general life and in scientific discourse. Let's explain what it is, why we use it, and then how we form the passive.

What Is 'The Passive'?

The passive is NOT a tense. Each tense has an active and passive form, which we call 'voice' but really means 'perspective'. Look at the following picture:

Figure 3-1

It is possible to describe the action in the picture from the viewpoint of the person 'doing' the action:

1. The man **is kissing** the woman.

But suppose we describe it from the viewpoint of the person 'receiving' the action:

2. The woman **is being kissed** by the man.

Notice that she is not doing anything; she is *passive*!

The verb in sentence (1) is in the *active voice*; the verb in (2) is in the *passive voice*. So the tense – present continuous – is the same, as we are talking about an action in the process of happening, at least in the picture. What are the elements in these sentences?

If we describe parts of the sentence by their meaning, the *agent* is the doer of the action and the *affected* is the 'receiver' of the action. In the active voice, the *agent* occupies the subject place in the sentence, while the *affected* occupies the object place. But in the passive voice, the *affected* is transformed from **object** to **subject**

The woman   is being kissed   by the man.

affected   agent

subject

Why is this potentially dangerous? The answer is that it allows us to delete the agent entirely, i.e., to keep the agent secret and still have a perfectly grammatical sentence, as:

-   The woman is being kissed.

Why Do We Use the Passive?

First of all, the agent is not always important. It may be the *affected* or the result of the action that is important, as in: *Hamlet was written in the 16th century.* As I mentioned before, sentences appear independently only in grammar books but in life, they are sensitive to the context. This passive sentence could conceivably be the response to the question, *When was Hamlet written?* or to a request, *Name one event of the 16th century.* Similarly, in scientific reporting, the emphasis theoretically, at least, is on the findings or ideas. Who did the research leading to these findings or proposed these ideas is supposed to be less important. This concept is discussed more thoroughly in Chapter 8, Review of the Literature.

The following sentences exemplify the main reasons for deleting the agent.

- Taxes are being raised.

- My wallet was stolen.

- A mistake has been made.

In the first case, we all know who is raising taxes; why add unnecessary information? In the second, we don't know who the agent is, so all we could say is that the agent was 'someone', which also doesn't add information. Sentence (3) demonstrates why using the passive is potentially manipulative. It was uttered by President Ronald Reagan when investigators discovered that the CIA had been shipping arms to Iran, in violation of U.S. law. This affair became known as 'Irangate'. By using passive voice, President Reagan managed to sidestep the question of who actually ordered this violation. In particular, he managed not to implicate himself. Although President Reagan really may not have remembered who the agent was, in general, people can use this tactic to evade responsibility.

When should you use the passive? In general, the passive should be avoided! It is more difficult for the brain to process a passive sentence than an active one. For instance, look at this created sentence:

- In the present work the visual response of several groups of children to distorted characters in a cartoon series was studied.

Isn't it easier to understand in the active voice, as in the following?

- In the present work we studied the visual response of several groups of children to distorted characters in a cartoon series.

In addition, there is a social reason for avoiding the passive in the Methods section when you describe how you treated people in your research, as in 'Participants were fed hamburgers.' The reason is not that the agent is deleted, since everyone knows that it is the author who performed the actions but because, according to the guidelines established by the APA (2001), people should not be described as passive objects. Chapter 9, Methods, provides more detail about dealing with this subject. On the other hand, passive voice is acceptable when explaining how you dealt with inanimate entities as in: *The data were analyzed by XYZ method.*

Does a scientist ever want to avoid naming the agent? What about statements such as: *It was thought that IQ is inherited*? Perhaps the author of this sentence lost the reference or wants to make sure that she is not counted among those who harbored these thoughts. Or, by a passive sentence, the role of other scientists (as agents) can be minimized as in *Smoking has been found to cause cancer.* (This choice is discussed further in Chapters 8 amd 11 in the section on hedging.)

Furthermore, a scientist can even want to evade responsibility, as in: *The rats were killed* or, as they used to euphemistically declare, *The rats were sacrificed after the experiment* rather than coldly confess *I killed the rats.*

How Do We Form the Passive?

Just as nouns are classified as count or uncount, verbs belong to one of two classes.

What is the grammatical difference between the verbs in columns (A) and (B)?

A	B
sleep	give
be	construct
jump	use

The correct answer is that the verbs in column A are *intransitive*, which means that they don't require an *affected* entity (object) to complete the statement. You can say, *Yesterday, I slept* or *jumped* and you have a complete sentence. Although the verb *to be* does not require an *affected* entity, it requires a complement, as in: *I was **late**.* In column B, however, if someone were to say *yesterday, I gave,* the listener would impatiently inquire *what?* Similarly, you cannot just *construct* or *use*; you must name an *affected* entity, as in *I constructed a questionnaire* or *I used the xyz program.* Such verbs are called *transitive.* When you look up *jump* in the dictionary, the entry will say *v.i,* (for *verb, intransitive*) while the entry for *give* will say *v.t.* (for *verb, transitive*). Thus, the verb can be changed to passive only if it is transitive, i.e., only if there is a slot for an *affected* entity in the sentence. Even if the verb is transitive, not every active sentence is acceptable in the passive. (*I have a cold* cannot be transformed to*A cold is had by me.*) Moreover, even when the passive form is grammatically acceptable, it is not appropriate in every context.

The sentences in the exercise below have been chosen for illustrating how to form the passive. In order to form the passive:

- Move the affected entity to the subject slot
- Add the verb *to be*; change it to the tense of the active verb
- Add the past participle of the verb, which is constant in **every** tense!

Table 3-3   Forming the Passive

Tense	To Be	Past Participle
Present simple	is/are	produced
Present continuous	is/are being	produced
Past simple	was/were	produced
Past continuous	was/were being	produced
Present perfect	has been	produced
Past perfect	had been	produced
Future	will be	produced
Recommended	should be	produced

For example:

In the passive form, the *affected* becomes the subject of the sentence and the verb *to be* is added.

Oranges   [to be]   [produces]
   ▾
subject
   ▾
affected

Since the main verb, *produces*, is in the present simple tense, we use the present simple of *to be*, i.e., **are**. We add the past participle *produced* regardless of the tense.

- **Oranges are** produced (by Florida).

(The agent – Florida – is added if relevant.)

Look at how other tenses are changed to the passive voice.

1. Smith has just produced a new play. (present perfect)

    Passive: Affected + to be + past participle

    A new play [to be + present perfect tense] [produced]

    Has been = present perfect form of *to be*.

    A new play has been produced by Smith.

2. The students produced **some good answers**.

    Passive: Affected + to be + past participle

    Some good answers [to be+ past simple] [produced]

    Were = past simple form of *to be*.

    Some good answers were produced by the students.

3. Jones will produce **a new textbook** next year.

    Passive: Affected + to be + past participle

    A new textbook [to be + future] [produced]

    A new textbook will be produced by Jones next year.

Task B: The Passive

Change the verbs in the following sentences to the passive voice. Remember not to change the tense. Decide when the agent should be named or should be deleted. Answers are at the end of this chapter.

1. Many researchers <u>have measured</u> the effect of punishment on achievement.

2. I <u>did not find</u> any significant differences among the various communities.

3. One <u>must take</u> care to control for [x].[Hint: 'care' is 'the affected' in this sentence.]

4. I <u>collected</u> the data.

5. Table II <u>depicts</u> the distribution of the activity in the whole sample.

6. People <u>have used</u> punishment effectively in laboratory settings.

7. We <u>can explain</u> the differences between these values by the fact that <u>we selected</u> our respondents from three different communities.

8. You <u>have to select</u> the sample from heterogeneous communities.

9. You <u>should not administer</u> punishment in front of others.

10. We do not know if the government <u>will accept</u> our recommendations.

Note that a passive form does not always convey a passive meaning. There is a passive meaning only when the subject is the entity affected by the action.

For instance, the following sentences are in the passive form (to be + past participle) but the meaning is not passive; there is no unnamed agent that has been deleted. You cannot add 'by someone' (agent) to any of them.

- They are interested in learning English.
- I was mistaken about the time.
- They were determined to finish the job.

Passive verbs can serve as adjectives, thereby compressing information in a sentence; see Chapter 9 on Methods, Compression.

Modals

The verbs in the examples we have discussed all indicate what the subject does, as in (1) or link the subject to the description as in (2) below:

1. unemployment leads to poverty

2. unemployment is a significant factor in causing poverty.

Since they carry the main meaning, let's call them *main* verbs. However, English has a few systems of auxiliary verbs, called *modals*, in which the author can add her opinion to the main verb. The two systems relevant for scientific writing are *possibility* and *recommendation*.

Possibility

By means of this modality system, the author can express how certain she is that the statement is true, e.g., she presents the statements in (1) and (2), above, as certainly true. But suppose she wants to indicate that it is *possible*, but not *certain*, that they are true. In that case, the author can say:

1. unemployment *may lead to* poverty

2. unemployment *may be* a significant factor

Although we speak of *certainty*, we mean *certainty* only as a grammatical construction. We discuss later, in Chapter 11, under Hedging, why an author might want to describe something as only possible even if she is certain.

The statements below express a range of possibility, from certain to uncertain. As is always true in using language, the correct choice of modal depends upon the context, which I've added.

- The garden *will* be very nice in the summer. (certain)
- It *should* rain tonight; there are lots of clouds in the sky.

(Some modals have more than one meaning. This example represents one of the meanings of *should*: to express a degree of certainty that an event will occur, not to make a recommendation.)

- It can rain tonight; this is the right season and temperature for it.
  (i.e., the potential exists)

- It *could* rain tonight, or tomorrow.
  (less certain than *can*, usually used when stating conditions)

The above situations refer to 'real' events, even if they have not occurred. However, we can refer to hypothetical events, as in:

- In subsequent research, [i.e., if someone did the research in the future], it *would* be interesting to compare the process of adaptation ... (Lehman, Wortman, & Williams, 1987).

In presenting these categories, I have followed the pedagogical custom of giving clear-cut examples. In fact, I try to confine my examples to rain because it is an unambiguous event. However, it should be stressed that in real life, the rules for modals are much more flexible than for tenses. While there is a hard and fast boundary between past and present, there are contexts in which the boundaries between *might*, *may*, and *should* and between *can* and *could* are more at the discretion of the author. For instance, the author who said 'what intervening mechanisms *might be* at work?' could just as well have said 'what intervening mechanisms *could/can/may be* at work?' I have intentionally not included all the possible categories of use for each modal, but you will see authentic examples at the end of this chapter.

The Negative

You will probably not need the negative form of these modals, but you might want to know them. I provide contexts in which the negative would be appropriate, in descending order of certainty:

1. According to the radio forecast, it *will not* rain tonight. (certain)

2. It *shouldn't* rain tonight; this is the dry season.

3. It *may not* rain today because there are only two clouds in the sky.

4. It *might not* rain today because there is only one cloud in the sky.

The Past

What about the past? How does the speaker indicate how certain he is that an event took place? Following are some ways to indicate the past.

Certain – The speaker expresses conviction

- It *rained* last night.

- It *did not rain* last night.

Less certain – The speaker expresses conjecture

- She *should have received* the letter by now; I mailed it a month ago.

- The experiment *should not have* failed; I had checked everything beforehand.

- She *may have received* the letter by now, since I sent it three days ago.

- She *may not have received* the letter because I may have misaddressed it.

- She *might have received* the letter by now, although I sent it only two days ago.

- She *might not have received* the letter since I sent it only two days ago.

- You say you spoke to a man from Mars? Such a thing *could* (*not*) *have* happened.

- This (hypothetical) solution *would have* worked in the past but it is impossible today.

- This (hypothetical) solution *would not have* worked in the past but it is possible today.

Recommendations

In a second system of modals, the author can show how strongly she recommends an action:

- Future epidemiological studies *should* seek additional information about anxiety symptoms … (Schneier, Johnson, Hornig, Leibowitz, & Weissman, 1992)

- Further studies of other populations *must* be performed. [created text]

The strength of that recommendation – weaker *should* or stronger *must* – just as the author's certainty of a fact, is entirely subjective. In other words, the choices depend on what the author wants to convey, rather than on some external 'reality'. For example, the sentence above could have said:

- 'Further studies of other populations *should* be performed' instead of *must*.

Although *should* and *must* are probably all that you will need, I provide a complete list of modals of recommendation, in case you come across them:

Stronger recommendation: both are on the same level

- Further studies *must* be performed.

- Further studies *have to* be performed.

Weaker recommendation: all are on the same level

- Therapists *should* focus on X.

- Therapists *ought to* focus on X.

- Therapists *need to* focus on X.

The Negative

The negative form of 'weaker recommendations' conforms to a regular pattern:

- Therapists *should not* focus on X.

- Therapists *ought not to* focus on X.

- Therapists *need to* focus on X. Negative form: In one variation, *to* is omitted: Therapists *need not* focus on X. In the other variation, *to* is retained: Therapists *don't need to* focus on X.

However, the negative form of 'stronger recommendations' is very tricky and illogical. **Note the difference**: the negative of ***must*** and ***have to*** are both ***do not have to***, i.e., you are not obligated to do something, e.g.,

- Physicians *must* perform operations under sterile conditions. However, they *do not have to* [it is not necessary to] perform examinations under sterile conditions.

Must not means that it is prohibited to (verb), as in:

- You *must not* smoke in the library. (Actually, you *don't have to* smoke at all!)

The Past

What does it mean to make a recommendation in the present or in the past tense?

In the present

- 'You *should* (*ought to*) read that book' means that you still can read that book, (if you want to)

But the 'past' really means that the action did **not** occur, as in:

- 'You *should have* (*ought to have*) read that book' means that you did *not* read it, although it was advisable to do so. So it is not really a 'past recommendation' but a reproach for *not* doing something (when addressed to human agents).

- You *needn't have* repeated the experiment. (It wasn't necessary but you did it.)

Again, ***must*** is in a class by itself. There is **no** past for ***must*** meaning past obligation. You would have to use the past of "have to":

- After the flood, the government *had to* provide emergency services.

Since ***must*** (in the sense of a very strong recommendation or obligation) is so tricky, I've provided Table 3-4 below:

Table 3-4   Strong Recommendation (*Must/Have To*)

	Present	Past
Positive	For experiments with humans, you **must/have to** obtain written permission.	To do this experiment, I **had to** obtain written permission.
Negative	For surveys, you **do not have to** obtain written permission.	To do this survey, I **did not have to** obtain written permission.

But even trickier is the use of ***must*** + 'the past'. While ***must*** in the present signifies a strong recommendation (*You must follow the law*) and ***must not*** signifies a strong prohibition (*You must not park on the sidewalk*), **must have** + verb signifies a strong conjecture.

- It *must have rained* last night. (I am almost certain because I see evidence of it, such as mud, puddles.)

- It *must not have rained* last night. (I am almost certain because the ground looks very dry.)

Using Modals

There are a few rules for using modals:

Possibility: modals have the same form for every subject, i.e., I/we/you/he, she, it/they may/might/can/would/could (+ verb)

Recommendation: Most modals have the same form for every subject, i.e., I/we/you/he, she, it/they must (+ verb)

> Exception: For *have to* and *need to*, the present tense follows the rule for main verbs in the third person:
>
> - He/she/the government *has to* reduce expenses.
>
> - He/she/the government *needs to* finish by May 1.

For both types of modals: the main verb is always in the base form for active sentences:

- I/we/you/he, she, the government/they should **finish** the work before May 1.

The main verb is always in the third form, the past participle, for passive sentences:

- The work should be **finished** by May 1.

In the past tense, all subjects take the same form of the verb: modal + have + past participle:

- I/we/you/he, she, the government/they **should have gone**

Some modals take **to** and some do not; there is no logical explanation for this!

- I must/will/may/can/could/might/should/would go, if invited.

But:

- I **have to** go

- I **ought to** go.

- I **need to** go.

Modals play a particularly important part in the Discussion section; see Chapter 11.

The Conditional

What is it?

In a sense, all the actions referred to in the above modal sentences are hypothetical, because they haven't occurred, but we have a special grammatical class that creates hypothetical statements and takes this form:

A	B
If this problem is solved,	*then we can move on to the next project.*

These are termed **conditional sentences**, consisting of a condition (A) and a result (or implication or conclusion) (B). You can expect the result to occur only if the condition is fulfilled, i.e., the result is dependent upon the condition. The word *then* in clause B is often deleted because it is understood. By the way, you can reverse A and B, and keep the meaning: '*We can move on to the next project, if this problem is solved.*' If life were simple, we would be finished now. However, conditions come in various strengths. Read sentences Type 1, Type 2, and Type 3 and try to guess the difference in the meaning among them.

- Type 1:   If you heat ice, [then] it melts.

  In this form, *if* can be replaced by *when*:

  When you heat ice, it melts

- Type 2:   If I get a fellowship, I will give a party.

Somewhere between (2) and (3) in strength is:

- Type 2a: If I *should get* a fellowship, I *will/would give* a party.

There is a famous conditional attributed to George Bernard Shaw. It seems he was irritating his dinner partner, Mrs. Astor. Finally, she said:

- Type 3:   If I were your wife, Mr. Shaw, I would give you poison

  to which he allegedly retorted:

  And, my dear lady, if I were your husband, I would take it!

To give a more academic example:

Result	Condition
Recycling would be increased	*if people were paid for the discarded containers.*

Notice the differences in tenses among Types 1, 2, and 3 below:

Type	A	B
Type 1	1. If you *heat* ice,	it *melts*
Type 2	2. If I *get* a fellowship,	I *will/might/may give* a party.
Type 3	3. If I *were* your wife,	I *would give* you poison.

In Type 1 above, the verbs in clause A and in B are both in the present simple tense; the *if* clause is not in the future tense, as in some languages.

In Type 2 above, the verb in clause A is in the present simple, but the verb in clause B is modified by a modal of certainty.

In Type 3 above, the verb in clause A is in the past tense but the verb in clause B is modified by a 'conditional' verb (would, could).

What do these differences mean? These different tenses do **not** express different times; remember, these events are all imaginary so there is no real past or present. However, they are used to express different attitudes of the speaker toward what she is saying.

In Type 1, the statement **always** is true; it is a generalization. In Type 2, the speaker feels that the result is **likely** to occur if the condition is met. It usually has to do with a specific instance or a specific grammatical subject. Type 2a is slightly more tentative than Type 2.

In Type 3, the speaker feels that the condition is either **not likely** ('*If I gave up smoking* …') or even contrary to fact ('*If I were a rich man* …'). By the way, for some historical reason, the correct form of *to be* in Type 3 is *were*: '*If he **were** able to….*' And NOT '*if he was able to* …'. From the following sentence, we know that the speaker feels that the possibility is very remote:

> If the elasticity of labour supply **were** larger, and that of savings lower, this could imply a higher rate of tax on capital income…. (Atkinson & Sandmo, 1980)

Sometimes the choice between types 2 and 3 can disclose the author's political opinion, such as:

- Type 2: If country X **wants** peace, she will ….
- Type 3: If country X **wanted** peace, she would ….

When Do We Use the Conditional?

Conditional sentences appear in different contexts, for example, in the Discussion section:

1. as a recommendation for future action:

   > If the majority of hard-core gang members **begin** associating with gangs at age 11 and drop out of school by the 10th grade, then programs **must target** elementary and middle-school students. (Molidor, 1996: 256)

2. as a logical conclusion:

> If the salience of a stimulus parameter **is** observable only within certain procedural constraints … the parameter **cannot be considered** to be a powerful one. (Columbo & Horowitz, 1986)

In addition, they explain mathematical formulae, especially in economics papers, as in:

> If [XX] **is** constant …, then the optimal tax formula **is** the familiar one. But if the social marginal valuation of income **falls** with w, this **tends** to increase the tax rate on goods…. (Atkinson & Stiglitz, 1976),

(which you will now recognize as a Type 1 condition) and

> If [XYZ] **were** equal to [ABC], then these equations would reduce to the standard formula (Atkinson & Sandmo, 1980),

(which you will now recognize as a Type 3 condition).

How Do We Use It?

Although the basics, above, will carry you through most of the time, you can introduce variations. For instance, a negative condition can be expressed as:

- We will go, *if* it *doesn't* rain

or

- We will go *unless* it rains.

Type 2 *if* can be replaced with *assuming that* or *provided that*:

- The work will be done, *assuming that/provided that* we find the necessary assistance.

Try composing some sentences using the structures below. Remember that you can make your condition or result negative, as well as positive. In informal speech, you can use contractions such as *would not = wouldn't* but not in formal writing.

Task C: The Conditional

Complete the following sentences for Types 2 & 3.

Type 1:

If (subject) (verb in present tense), then (subject) (verb in present tense).

- If they *are* asked to reply, most people *cooperate*.

Type 2:

If (subject) (verb in present tense), then (subject) (*will* or other modal + verb).

- If I *get* a fellowship, I *will/might/may give* a party.

1. If the world population continues to grow, we will/might/may/could

_____.

2. _____, if we ignore global warming.

3. _____, _____

Type 3:

If (subject) (verb in past tense), then (subject) (*would/could/might* + verb).

1. If I *were* President, I *would* _____.

2. If scientists *found* a cure for cancer, _____.

3. We *could* prevent wars, if _____.

There is always one more thing. In the remote possibility that you will need it, I include Type 4. Can anything be even more hypothetical than the sentences above? The answer is yes. If you look back, you will notice that we could conceivably add the word *now* to all these sentences, e.g., 'if I were President (now) ....' But suppose you want to talk about hypothetical events in the past; instead of *now*, you need a whole new sentence structure, as in:

- Type 4:   If I *had known* it would take 30 years, I *wouldn't have attempted* to earn a Ph.D.

To put such a structure in a scientific context, suppose you do a pilot study to see if people return your questionnaires. If the response rate is favorable, you might say:

- If the response rate **had been** less than 60%, I **would have offered** to pay them.

The positive Type 4 structure means that the condition was **not** realized and the result **did not** occur, i.e., the response rate **was not** less than 60% and you **didn't** offer to pay the people

If the response rate is unfavorable, you then have to offer a financial incentive. Then after the study, you say:

- If I **had not offered** to pay them, there **would not have been** a response rate of 60%.

The negative Type 4 structure means that the condition **was** realized (you had to offer to pay the people) and the result **did** occur, i.e., the response rate **was** at least 60%

Putting It All Together

You can see below how the tenses, active and passive voice, and modality are integrated in an actual Introduction; notice that different tenses can be used in different clauses even within the same sentence, since the tense in each clause must be chosen according to the meaning of the clause.

Religion, Disability, Depression, and the Timing of Death

When reference is made to Durkheim's interest in the link between religion and individual or group well-being, the source is nearly always *Suicide* .... In *Suicide*, Durkheim ... considers the life – preserving functions of religion to be indistinguishable from those of the family. .... Researchers typically find support for the *Suicide* model: the concrete and material support that can be offered by members of a religious congregation is increasingly being recognized as a social resource .... Religious groups offer ... the intimacy of close ties that can easily penetrate the private sphere, though these benefits may vary from one religious group to another .... Religious – group membership may also provide an incentive for rehabilitation and recovery because it offers ... a public role to return to ....

Durkheim's appreciation of the complexity of religious experience apparently increased during the 18 years between *Suicide* and [*EFRL*]. ... The relevance of what in [*EFRL*] has become 'a system of ideas' .... The religious impulse is to separate the body ... from the soul ....

Seeing the body as simply a material envelope ... could be an increasingly comforting perception ... Thus, any examination of the relevance of religion to health must consider its particular role in situations of serious illness and suffering .... And one might expect a heightened sense of religious introspection. ...

Religious-group membership has usually been included in studies of the impact of social networks on mortality, and it has frequently been found to have independent protective effects ....

The Durkheimian framework … allows us to predict that some religious groups <u>should be</u> more <u>protected</u> than others, that is, that Catholics and Jews, with their tightly integrated societies, <u>should derive</u> greater benefits than Protestants….

If religious – group involvement <u>is</u> related to better health, what intervening mechanisms <u>might be</u> at work? ….

On the other hand … we <u>are</u> left with a protective effect that <u>would appear</u> to be more uniquely religious. This <u>would necessitate</u> the move from *Suicide* to *EFRL* with its more complex consideration of the facets of religious experience. …

Hypotheses

…. The analysis of disability is based on the hypothesis that religious involvement <u>will have</u> a broad protective effect against disability. Among those who are not disabled, religious involvement <u>will be associated</u> with a lesser likelihood of decline of functional ability.

[Idler found that] public religious involvement <u>was associated</u> with better functional ability … and that disabled men who <u>were</u> more privately religious <u>were</u> less likely to be depressed. (Idler & Kasl, 1992: 1052–1057)

In Table 3-5, below, notice that the three uses of the present simple tense that we discussed above are illustrated in column 2, active:

1. *Researchers typically <u>find</u> support for the Suicide model*: habitual action

2. *Durkheim … <u>considers</u> …* —Durkheim is dead but his work still lives and is considered relevant;

3. *The religious impulse <u>is</u> to separate the body…* —This idea is presented as a general social phenomenon that is always true.

Table 3-5 Summary of Verb Usage

Tense	Static	Continuous
Present		
Non-perfective		
Active	1. Researchers typically <u>find</u> support for the *Suicide* model: 2. Durkheim … <u>considers</u> 3. The religious impulse <u>is</u> to separate the body	
Passive	When reference <u>is made</u> to Durkheim's interest	the … support <u>is</u> increasingly <u>being recognized</u> as a social resource

Perfective		
Active	what in *EFRL* <u>has become</u> 'a system of ideas'	
Passive	Religious-group membership <u>has</u> usually <u>been included</u> in studies	
Past		
Non-perfective		
Active	Durkheim's appreciation … <u>increased</u> during the 18 years	
Passive (from Discussion section)	Our measure of public religiousness <u>was intended</u> to tap the congregational dimension …	
Future		
Non-perfective		
Active	religious involvement <u>will have</u> a broad protective effect	
Passive (form)	religious involvement <u>will be associated</u> with …	

Now I'll highlight the modality system in this passage:

> …. Researchers typically find support for the Suicide model: the concrete and material support that **can be offered** by members of a religious congregation …. Religious groups offer … the intimacy of close ties that **can** easily **penetrate** the private sphere, though these benefits **may vary** from one religious group to another …. Religious – group membership **may** also **provide** an incentive for rehabilitation and recovery because it offers … a public role to return to ….
>
> Seeing the body as simply a material envelope … **could be** an increasingly comforting perception … Thus, any examination of the relevance of religion to health **must consider** its particular role in situations of serious illness and suffering …. And one **might expect** a heightened sense of religious introspection. …
>
> The Durkheimian framework … allows us to predict that some religious groups **should be** more **protected** than others, that is, that Catholics and Jews, with their tightly integrated societies, **should derive** greater benefits than Protestants….
>
> If religious – group involvement is related to better health, what intervening mechanisms **might be** at work? ….

On the other hand, to the extent that these intervening mechanisms do not eliminate the association, we are left with a protective effect that **would appear** to be more uniquely religious. This **would necessitate** the move from *Suicide* to *EFRL* with its more complex consideration of the facets of religious experience. ...

Hypotheses

.... The analysis of disability is based on the hypothesis that religious involvement **will have** a broad protective effect against disability. Among those who are not disabled, religious involvement **will be associated** with a lesser likelihood of decline of functional ability.

We can categorize these modals as:

Recommendation

- any examination of the relevance of religion to health <u>must consider</u> ...

Possibility

The authors express *certainty* in stating their hypotheses:

1. religious involvement **will have** a broad protective effect against disability.

2. religious involvement **will be associated** with a lesser likelihood of decline of functional ability.

The authors offer reasons justifying their hypotheses; they show these are conjecture through modals expressing various degrees of possibility.

1. these benefits **may vary** from one religious group to another

2. one **might expect** a heightened sense of religious introspection. ...

3. Catholics and Jews ... **should derive** greater benefits than Protestants

4. some religious groups **should be** more **protected** than others,

5. what intervening mechanisms **might be** at work?

6. the intimacy of close ties that **can** easily **penetrate** the private sphere, material support that **can be offered** by members of a religious congregation

7. Seeing the body as simply a material envelope ... **could be** an increasingly comforting perception

8. we are left with a protective effect that **would appear** to be more uniquely religious....

Conditional Sentence

- If religious – group involvement <u>is</u> related to better health, what intervening mechanisms **might be** at work?

You will see that modality is used extensively, for different purposes, in the Discussion. See Chapter 11.

Task D: Review of Grammar (and a few other points)

The following passages written by students include mistakes in nouns and verbs, as well as other problems. As a final 'exam', can you correct them and other errors you see? Among the items to check:

Are the nouns in their correct form (count/uncount)?

Are the verbs in the correct tenses?

Are the verbs in the present simple tense conjugated appropriately for third person?

Are the pronouns correct?

Should any articles (*a, the*) be added or removed?

1. The research I am doing right now focuses on children that their parents are drug and alcohol addicted. The purpose of the study is to analyze patterns of attachment and psychosocial adjustment of these children. Empirical evidences has support the view that growing up with an addicted parents increase the likelihood of experiencing disruption in emotional, social, and interpersonal functioning. A lot of researches have been done concerning the addiction circumstances [probably means 'environment'] but till the 80's there were no attention to the implications of growing up in addicted family.

2. My proposal is to research the subjective assessment of the retirement and how this assessment affect on the sense of subjective adjustment. The reason that this issue is important flows from the fact that the population of the aging people increase all the time. Also, the range of the ages of the employees become smaller, and people now retire from work since age 55. These two phenomenon cause a great increase in the number of the retirees and even though retirement is a developmental event, people always feel not prepare to deal with. According to the theoretical and research literature, retirement issues investigated a lot, but with quantitative tools and with models that fit young people, and most of the time understand retirement as a stressful event.

3. Given this parameters we analyze the effects of different tax regimes by simulate the market equilibrium under different regimes. Specifically, we investigate the effect of three possible reforms. The first one is making taxation uniform for all cars from different country origin. The second is 20% increase in tax, while the third is across the board reduction of 30% of tax.

If you would like more explicit guidelines, see Answers to Tasks (D).

Answers to Tasks

Task B: The Passive

1. The effect of punishment on achievement <u>has been measured</u> by many researchers.

2. No significant differences <u>were found</u> among the various communities. (The agent, *by me*, is not necessary if it is clear that you are writing up your own research)

3. Care <u>must be taken</u> to control for [x]. (When a sentence is in the form of instructions or a command, *you* is understood.)

4. The data <u>were collected</u>. (Again, the agent is clear; see #2. The tricky part here was to remember that the word *data* is plural.)

5. The distribution of the activity in the whole sample <u>is depicted</u> in Table II.

6. Punishment <u>has been used</u> effectively in laboratory settings.

7. The differences between these values <u>can be explained</u> by the fact that our respondents <u>were selected</u> from three different communities.

8. The sample <u>has to be selected</u> from heterogeneous communities. (The agent *you* is unnecessary; see # 3.)

9. Punishment <u>should not be administered</u> in front of others.

10. We do not know if our recommendations <u>will be accepted</u> (by the government)

Task C: The conditional

Since there are an infinite number of possibilities, I haven't provided answers. Just check your answer with the tenses in the models I've provided.

Task D: Review of Grammar

Follow the guidelines below the passage for making corrections:

Example 1

The research I am doing right now focuses on children (1) <u>that their</u> parents are drug and alcohol addicted. The purpose of the study is to analyze patterns of attachment and psychosocial adjustment of these children. Empirical (2) <u>evidences</u> (3) has <u>support</u> the view that growing up with (4) <u>an addicted parents</u> (5) <u>increase</u> the likelihood of experiencing disruption in emotional, social, and interpersonal functioning. (6) <u>A lot of researches</u> (7) <u>have</u> been done concerning the environment of addiction but till the 80's [1980's] (8) <u>there were no attention</u> to the implications of growing up in (9) addicted family.

How to make corrections:

1. use the pronoun for showing that 'parents belong to the children'

2. *evidence* is an uncount noun, i.e., never plural

3. in the present perfect, the verb should be in the third form (past participle)

4. is it one *parent* or more than one?

5. now change the verb to fit the subject (*parent* or *parents*)

6. Ow! Scientists never have *a lot of* anything; besides, *research* is an uncount noun, i.e., never plural

7. now change the verb *have* to fit the subject *research*

8. *attention* is an uncount noun, i.e., never plural; change the verb to fit the subject.

9. *family* is a count noun; therefore it cannot be left bare – you need to indicate if you are talking about one *family* or many *families*.

Example 2

My proposal is to research the subjective assessment of (1) <u>the</u> retirement and how this assessment (2) <u>affect on</u> the sense of subjective adjustment. (3) <u>The reason that this issue is important flows from the fact that</u> the population of (4) <u>the</u> aging people (5) <u>increase</u> (6) <u>all the time</u>. (7) <u>Also, the range of the ages of the employees become smaller, and people now retire from work since age 55.</u> These (8) <u>two phenomenon</u> (9) <u>cause</u> a great increase in the number of (10) <u>the</u> retirees and even though retirement is a developmental event, people (11) <u>always feel not prepare</u> (12) <u>to deal with</u>. According to the theoretical and research [empirical] literature, retirement issues (13) <u>investigated</u> (14) <u>a lot</u>, but with quantitative tools and with models that fit young people, and most of the time (15) <u>understand</u> retirement as a stressful event.

How to make corrections:

1. *retirement* is a general, not specific, noun

2. make the verb fit the subject (singular) *retirement* (and remove *on*)

3. This is a long way of saying something; can you change it by using *because*?

4. *aging people* is a general, not a specific noun phrase

5. & 6. use the tense that shows that the phenomenon is going on now, in which case *all the time* is not necessary.

7. This is a long way of saying *People are retiring now at age 55.*

8. If there are two of them, you must use the plural form of *phenomenon*; see Chapter 2, Table 2-2.

9. Again, if you want to emphasize that this is a current phenomenon, change the tense to present continuous.

10. Again, you don't mean specific retirees

11. *people do not always feel* + use the past participle for *prepare*

12. *to deal with* takes an object; add the correct pronoun.

13. Change the tense to present perfect to show that you are speaking of research as of today. Then remember that *retirement issues* cannot *investigate* anything, i.e., someone has to do it to them. Therefore the verb should be in the passive form.

14. See #6 in example 1, above. Scientists never have *a lot of'* anything.

15. It is not clear who or what is the subject for *understand*.

Example 3

Given (1) <u>this parameters</u> we analyze the effects of different tax regimes by (2) <u>simulate</u> the market equilibrium under different regimes. Specifically, we investigate the effect of three possible reforms. The first one (3) <u>is making</u> taxation uniform for all cars from (4) <u>different country origin</u>. The second is (5) <u>20% increase in tax</u>, while the third is (6) <u>across the board reduction of 30% of tax</u>.

How to make corrections:

1. Is it one *parameter* or more than one?

2. after *by* you must use the noun form of the verb, i.e., *simulating*

3. this sentence expresses a rule for taxation not a current phenomenon. Change the tense accordingly.

4. if they are *different* there must be more than one country. You would also need to add *of* before *origin*.

5. & 6. both *increase* and *reduction* are count nouns; therefore, you need to add the indefinite article before the noun phrase (underlined).

Chapter 4

Shaping Sentences and Paragraphs

Now let's discuss how to build sentences with the nouns and verbs.

Keep Elements in Order

The nouns become subjects and objects; in one type of sentence, verbs tell what the subject does. If the verb is intransitive, we have a complete sentence with only a subject and verb: Smith died. If the verb is transitive, we need to add an object, as in: Smith writes books. The usual order, as shown by the sentence is: Subject–Verb–Object.

In the second type of sentence, the verb links the subject to some kind of description, termed a Complement, as in 'Smith (S) *is* (V) tired/in the next room/a colleague of Jones' (C). In this type, the usual order is: Subject–Verb–Complement.

However, life is never so simple. In formal writing, we add many phrases to give extra information. We might want to modify the subjects and objects (tell more about them), by adding adjectives (one or many words):

- Smith, *who hasn't had a vacation all year*, is tired.

Or we might want to modify the verb, by adding adverbs (again, one or many words):

- Smith *writes* books very quickly.
- Smith *writes* in his office.
- Smith *writes* books by dictating to his secretary.

Some types of adverbs may also be placed at the beginning of the sentence, as in:

- By dictating to his secretary, Smith avoids writing on the computer.
- In order to keep his job, Smith writes a book a year.

You may add anything you want as long as you remember to keep information units together, i.e., keep the modifiers in immediate contact with the elements they modify. If not, you might wind up with something like this:

- Dressed in her pajamas, the police arrested the prostitute

when you really mean:

- The police arrested the prostitute dressed in her pajamas.

The phrase *dressed in her pajamas* is a modifier of *the prostitute*.

When the modifier is in the wrong place, it is called, oddly enough, *a misplaced modifier*.

Now I made up the above example, but here is an actual example, from an advertisement that urged readers to:

> Prevent damage to garden and lawns from burrowing rodents with … the electronic stake that emits vibration and sound that's intensely annoying to underground rodents **up to 100 feet in diameter.** (Rawdon, 1990)

Can you imagine a rodent that is "*up to 100 feet in diameter*"? I think that the author actually meant to modify the range in which the sound is emitted:

> Prevent damage to garden and lawns from burrowing rodents with … the electronic stake that emits vibration and sound **up to 100 feet in diameter, which is** intensely annoying to underground rodents.

Similarly, here is an example from a student's essay:

> **Often neglected, overlooked or not measured at all**, our work demonstrates the importance of this term and the high values involved.

Did the author intend to use "*Often neglected, overlooked or not measured at all*" to modify "*our work*"? Where do you think it belongs? The most chilling example of a misplaced modifier is provided by Pechenik (1987), from an article about the ethics of *in vitro* fertilization:

- What is it that bothers us about the egg and sperm of that couple who died in Australia sitting on ice?

Where does *sitting on ice* belong? (Actually, *sitting on ice* is hardly a scientific way to describe eggs and sperm. The author is undoubtedly speaking about *frozen* sperm and eggs.)

- What is it that bothers us about the egg and sperm, now sitting on ice, that belongs to that couple who died in Australia?

Keep Elements Parallel

Here, a student tries to describe a painting on an archeological artifact she found:

> The scene represents seated women; one is spinning, holding a distaff and a spindle, and the other holds a small frame. This way of spinning has not changed over the centuries as can be seen from base paintings, from Roman gravestones, and continues to this day on the island of Crete.

In these sentences, some of the grammatical structures are not parallel (underlined):

> (1) The scene represents seated women; <u>one is spinning</u>, holding a distaff and a spindle, and <u>the other holds a small frame</u>. (2) This way of spinning has not changed over the centuries as can be seen <u>from vase paintings, from Roman gravestones, and continues to this day on the island of Crete</u>.

In sentence (1), the word *and* joins a description of two women:

- one is spinning, holding a distaff and a spindle,

and

- the other holds a small frame.

While the subjects *one* and *the other* are parallel (both pronouns), the verb tenses *is spinning* and *holds* are not parallel. You would have to say either:

- One spins and the other holds a small frame

or

- One is spinning and the other is holding a small frame

Since they are shown in the middle of an activity, the present continuous seems more appropriate here.

Similarly, in (2), we have a lack of parallelism in:

- vase paintings, [= noun phrase]
- Roman gravestones, [= noun phrase]

and

- continues to this day on the island of Crete. [= verb + adverbs]

In order to make it parallel, and retain the information, the third element needs to be changed to: a noun phrase, e.g.:

- contemporary spinning on the island of Crete.

If the author wants to emphasize the continuation of this traditional method, she could write:

- This way of spinning has not changed over the centuries, as can be seen from ancient vase paintings and Roman gravestones, and contemporary spinning on the island of Crete.

Avoid Heavy Sentences

By *heavy*, I am not referring to the number of words, but the amount of information. Scientific writing involves sentences that are packed with information. It is too hard for the brain to absorb it all in one try. If readers find they have to go back and re-read the sentence, they may soon lose patience with the text, or the writer.

Ponder this sentence by a budding social worker:

> Hence, it is hypothesized that, since the supervisee will perceive the supervisor as more judgemental, because of the dominance of the evaluative component in supervision, she will be less authentic in her relationship with the supervisor, whereas the client will perceive the therapist as less judgemental, because of the absence or the weakness of the evaluative component in therapy (compared to supervision) and thus, will be able to be more authentic in her relationship with the therapist.

There are many ways to determine that it is too heavy. For one, there are five clauses (verb + subject) in it, like fifty pounds of apples hanging on one branch. You could also say that there are seven units of information (conveniently marked off by commas). However, the easier rule is the Lewin Principle. Read the sentence aloud. If you have to stop to breathe more than twice, the sentence is too heavy. I suggest breaking this sentence up into smaller sentences even if it involves repeating a few words to make it comprehensible. The sentence seems to balance on the word whereas, so I would make the first break there. Since *whereas* can join only two clauses, I have to use a different connector.

> Hence, it is hypothesized that, since the supervisee will perceive the supervisor as more judgemental, because of the dominance of the evaluative component in supervision, she will be less authentic in her relationship with the supervisor
>
> [whereas] **In contrast**, the client will perceive the therapist as less judgemental, because of the absence or the weakness of the evaluative component in therapy (compared to supervision) and thus, will be able to be more authentic in her relationship with the therapist.

Also, I suggest putting the 'causes' in chronological order, and not as written i.e.:

- [cause A] the dominance of the evaluative component in supervision,

- [results in] the supervisee will perceive the supervisor as more judgemental,

- [which results in] she will be less authentic in her relationship with the supervisor

can be rewritten as:

> Hence, because of the dominance of the evaluative component in supervision, it is hypothesized that the supervisee will perceive the supervisor as more judgemental. Therefore, she will be less authentic in her relationship with the supervisor.

Fortunately, in my experience, the problem of writing sentences that are too short has not occurred.

Avoid Ambiguity

Following are sentences that I haven't been able to figure out till this day:

- X is thought to be more unambiguous ....

Something is either unambiguous or not. Does the author mean *X is clearer*?

or, more horrible, double negatives:

- Literature concerning very young patients with infection often gives the impression that [X symptom] is not infrequently absent in these patients.

Do the patients get X symptom or don't they?

Punctuate Punctiliously

You might think that rules of punctuation are minor issues.[1] You have enough on your hands and editors would not mind adding a comma here and there. However, in certain cases, the punctuation changes the meaning of the statement. For instance, how would you punctuate the following sentence, said by a young lady to her date, who has stopped to park in a lonely spot?

- Oh no John please don't stop

Well, there are two ways:

- Oh, no, John! Please don't! Stop!

- Oh, no, John, please! Don't stop!

It is possible that a young man can be accused of rape, depending upon how he interprets the punctuation.

Although it may not lead to a criminal trial, in scientific writing, incorrect punctuation may lead to misunderstanding, as illustrated by the title of a popular book "*Eats, shoots and leaves*" (Truss, 2003). You would reasonably think this book is about a criminal who finished a meal in a restaurant before he committed murder. It's actually about the importance of punctuation. The author of the sentence meant to describe the eating habits of a panda and should have written: *Eats shoots and leaves.*

Both examples also show that punctuation in writing is necessarily to replace signals we give when we speak. If we were referring to a panda, we wouldn't pause between *eats* and *shoots*, whereas if we were referring to a hungry murderer, we would pause (an oral comma) after *eats* and *shoots*. Think of a period at the end of a sentence as a red light, a long wait. A semi-colon is equivalent to a stop sign; you can go ahead after you've stopped and seen that the road is clear; a comma is a very short stop, such as a yellow 'give right of way' stop. Other marks may be just convention, e.g., why must there be a comma after *e.g.* in the middle of a sentence?

It is also true that the rules of punctuation, like spelling, vary between British and American authors, and have changed over time. I use American rules, not because of "American imperialism" but because the US contributes 31% of mainstream journal articles, while the UK contributes 8%. (Gibbs, 1995) Secondly, since I was in school, the tendency has been to omit many commas and periods. We used to place a comma after words that came before the subject, as in '*Apparently, she was wrong*' and after abbreviations such as '*Mr.*'. However, publishers have obviously found it cheaper to omit them so we can't fight that custom. Of course, you must keep the comma or period where omitting them would cause confusion.

I have tried to limit the discussion below to the 'bottom line' about punctuation, especially problems that could lead to misunderstanding.

1. **Dashes — — and parentheses ( )** are almost interchangeable. They are both used to set off information that is not an integral part of the sentence, which means that the main idea of the sentence can be understood without the words within the dashes or parentheses, e.g.,

    - It is because of the disruptive potential of scandals that sundry actors—from private citizens, to the press, to prosecutors—routinely resort to them for opportunistic as well as moral purposes. (Adut, 2005: 244)

It would be acceptable and clear to use parentheses in this case:

- It is because of the disruptive potential of scandals that sundry actors (from private citizens, to the press, to prosecutors) routinely resort to them for opportunistic as well as moral purposes (adapted from Adut, 2005: 244)

or commas:

- It is because of the disruptive potential of scandals that sundry actors, from private citizens, to the press, to prosecutors, routinely resort to them for opportunistic as well as moral purposes (adapted from Adut, 2005: 244)

2. **Inverted commas, commonly called quotation marks, double "xxx" or single 'xxx'** (depending upon the style manual of your target journal). The absence of inverted commas is the second case in which punctuation could land you in court. All direct quotes must be signaled as such, and the appropriate citation given. Inverted commas do not serve only as quotation marks but are also used to signal that the author does not agree, as I did when I used the term "American imperialism", above.

3. **Ellipsis ...** missing information is signified by three dots, four if it is at the end of the sentence. This is the third case that could get you in trouble. Some authors tend to quote the part of the review they liked:

- Jones stated that this book is exceptional ...

which Jones did say, but the complete sentence, including the part which was omitted, should read:

- Jones stated that this book is exceptional in its total neglect of any studies after 1980.

4. **Brackets [ ]** are used to indicate a parenthesis within a parenthesis, as in Crowson, Thoma, and Hestevold (2005: 573):

- Ironically, these authors largely used measures of authoritarianism (e.g., Altemeyer's [1996, 1998] RWA Scale, California F-Scale [Adorno et al., 1950/1982], Social Dominance Orientation Scale [Sidanius & Pratto, 1999])

More importantly, brackets are necessary within a quotation to indicate that the author who is quoting has added information that was not in the original source, as in the statement I quoted in Chapter 1:

Whenever a scientist communicates, even the most mundane and seemingly innocuous descriptions, he [she] is persuading his [her] audience, literally commanding them to adopt his [her] point of view. (Weimar, 1977: 1)

Weimar wrote this before the revolution that required equal representation for the feminine gender. When I quoted it, above, I added the female pronouns.

I should add that if you want to leave the original text, even with infractions of rules, you—the quoting author—should add the word *sic* (Latin that means 'that's the way it was') in brackets, as in:

> Whenever a scientist communicates, even the most mundane and seemingly innocuous descriptions, he [sic] is persuading his audience, literally commanding them to adopt his point of view (Weimar, 1977: 1).

5. A **colon :** points to what follows such as details or a quote; it should not be used to join two sentences. Examples:

- The rates are: 60%, 75%, 80%.

- A noun is the name of anything: a person, place, thing, quality, idea or activity.

6. The **semi-colon ;**

The semi-colon has two important functions.

Firstly, it makes the connection between two sentences stronger, as in:

- It was raining; however, we went on the picnic.

Secondly, a semi-colon separates clauses that already have commas in them, and prevents confusion. For instance, how many people are represented in the following list?

- the President the Republican candidate the minority leader the Democratic candidate the former president the Senator from New York

To indicate that six people are included, I could just use commas:

- the President, the Republican candidate, the minority leader, the Democratic candidate, the former president, the Senator from New York

However, to indicate that only three people are meant, we would invoke the worthy semi-colon. This would mean that the President IS the Republican candidate and so on:

- the President, the Republican candidate; the minority leader, the Democratic candidate; the former president, the Senator from New York

You will find the semi-colon when more than one publication is cited in a text, as in:

- (Jones, 1968; Gilbert, 1977; Smith, 1999).

7. The **comma ,**

You are undoubtedly already familiar with many of the common purposes the comma serves, such as separating items in a series:

- She bought oranges, tomatoes, and cucumbers for dinner.

And separating clauses:

- While they were eating dinner, the phone rang.

However, there is one case in which the comma changes the meaning of the entire sentence. This is when the 'who clause' is part of the subject (a, below) and when it is not part of the subject but just added information, (b, below).

a. University employees who work after 6 p.m. will be served dinner.

b. University employees, who work after 6 p.m., will be served dinner.

The subject of sentence (a, above) is: *University employees who work after 6 p.m.* Only they (and not people who work until 5 p.m.) will be served dinner.

The subject of sentence (b, above) is *University employees*, which means that all those lucky people will be served dinner. People have had fun showing different examples of this use of the comma. Which one was written by an obvious sexist?

a. Women who are emotionally unstable should not be elected to public office.

b. Women, who are emotionally unstable, should not be elected to public office.

In the following examples, which one shows that everyone failed the test?

a. The students, who failed the test, blamed the teacher.

b. The students who failed the test blamed the teacher

However, as you remember from Chapter 2, Nouns and Pronouns, you can use *who* only when referring to humans. When referring to non-humans, you must use *that* when the clause is part of the subject.

For instance, if you want to show that *experience 100 atmospheres of pressure* refers only to certain fish, use *that* as in:

- Fish that live at a depth of 1000m. experience 100 atmospheres of pressure.

Use *which*, separated from the subject by a comma, to show that the clause *experience 100 atmospheres of pressure* is not part of the subject.

The following sentence says all fish live at a depth of 1000m, which, although not true, makes for an interesting example:

- Fish, which live at a depth of 1000m, experience 100 atmospheres of pressure.

Now for some examples from real life, showing that the misuse of the comma changes the sense of the sentence.

1. *Another important aspect of my plan deals with the privatization of firms, which are owned by the government.

This means that all firms are owned by the government, which is untrue.

2. *No one defined humanism until Eugenio Garin in Italy and Hans Baron, first in Germany and after the rise of Hitler in the United States … (Rabil, 1988: 141).

In this sentence, the absence of commas changes the history of the whole world!

3. * … the cognitive information processes, that lead to the final estimation (which we can call the cognitive strategy)

The author either means '… *the cognitive information processes, which lead to the final estimation (which we can call the cognitive strategy)*. This means that **all** cognitive information processes lead to …

or:

… the cognitive information processes that lead to the final estimation (which we can call the cognitive strategy). She is going to speak only of some cognitive information processes, i.e., the ones that lead to ….

Task A: Sexist Commas

Punctuate the following sentence, (1) as a very macho man would, and (2) as a very feminist woman would:

- A woman without her man is nothing.

(Answers at the end of the chapter)

Caution

On the other hand, it is incorrect to sprinkle commas wherever one feels like it. Like everything else, their placement is regulated by rules. Commas cannot solve the problem of heavy sentences, for instance. Moreover, there should be **no** comma between the subject and verb/complement in the same clause, as in:

- *This work, shows that the relationship between X and Y is complicated.

What the author means is: This work shows that the relationship between X and Y is complicated.

8. ☹ The **apostrophe** ' should not be used except for indicating the possessive, as in: *Durkheim's work*. Contractions (e.g., doesn't) should not be used in an academic article.

There is one exception to the possessive rule. The possessive of *it* is *its*. For some reason, the word *it's* has crept in like a virus and should be treated as such—totally exterminated from our writing. *It's* stands for *it is* or *it has*. Please remember these examples:

a. It's been (i.e., it has been) a long time since I've seen you.

b. The dog wagged **its** tail.

☹⚠ Even English speakers are beginning to put apostrophes where they don't belong (☹☹☹*potatoe's). Do not catch this disease!

Paragraphs

I want to emphasize that sentences do not exist in isolation, as I often see from initial drafts as in the following example:

> This is my first sentence, which I am writing to show you what not to do under any circumstances.
> This is my second sentence, which I am writing to show you what not to do under any circumstances.
> This is my third sentence, which I am writing to show you what not to do under any circumstances.

When you write like that, you are breaking up the ideas not only on the page, but in the reader's mind. You are telling the reader that these ideas are not connected. Instead, remember that each sentence is part of a train of thought comprising a paragraph. On the other hand, it is over generalizing to say that every paragraph consists of a main idea and all the details about that idea; that could describe your whole text. However, a paragraph should contain related sentences, even if there is not an ideal main sentence at the beginning. Look at a printed page in a journal and determine how many sentences are in the typical paragraph. What is the average number of paragraphs on a page? In general, the length of the paragraph, like the length of each sentence, is a function of the level of the audience, with sentences and paragraphs shorter in more popular media. Novice writers tend to think that each new idea necessitates a new paragraph like this literature review, adapted:

> Forsyth (1979) found nurses had moderate to high empathy and that scores were higher for baccalaureate nurses when compared with diploma level nurses.

> Iwasiw and Olston (1985) found it was baccalaureate prepared nurses who were more empathic.

> Anderson and Gerrard (1984) found that first year students who participated in a comprehensive interpersonal skills course were more empathic than a control group that had received no training.

> Daniels et al., (1988) demonstrated the efficacy of a microcounselling program for teaching therapeutic communication skills to nurses.

All these sentences can be legitimately bound together by a general opening statement (sometimes called a *controlling idea*) such as the author has done:

> It has long been acknowledged that interpersonal communication, helping, and counselling skills are a fundamental component of the nurses role and essential prerequisites for quality nursing care [citations]. (Sellick, 1991)

Of course, the author also did not write the monotonous sentences above. I did, to show how orphan sentences look. You will find guidelines in Chapter 8 for organizing your Review of Literature and in Chapter 6, for connecting parts of the text.

Answers to Task A: Sexist Commas

1. According to a male chauvinist:

    A woman without her man is nothing.

2. According to a female chauvinist

    A woman: without her, man is nothing.

Notes:

[1] 'Mariner 1, the American rocket bound for Venus a few years ago, had to be blasted apart when it began veering off course. *The Book of Lists II* says that an investigation revealed that the erratic behaviour had been caused by the omission of a hyphen from the flight's computer programme. The lack of this single piece of punctuation cost U.S. taxpayers $18.5 million'. (Mariner I, 1988)

Chapter 5

Being Concise

Unlike novelists, authors of scientific texts are told to write concisely. What does this mean? In her writing manual, Beth Luey (1995: 9) advised that *'For the purposes of good academic writing, writing well is writing clearly and succinctly.'* She then realized that that sentence could have been made more concise thusly:

'Good academic writing is clear and succinct.' However, I wouldn't say that conciseness overrides all other considerations. There is a happy medium. You might feel that the original sentence made a stronger impact as a more memorable directive.

One of the main differences between oral and written language is that the former is very repetitive. That stands to reason, since oral language must be heard and committed to memory. Repetition guards against lapses in each step. So someone giving a recipe for apple pie to a friend over the telephone might say:

- First, slice the apples. Next, butter a baking dish. You have to pack the apple slices closely in the dish. Remember not to cover the dish. Put it in the oven. Bake it for an hour.

However, the same information could be given concisely, without any loss of information as:

- Pack sliced apples closely in a buttered baking dish and bake uncovered for one hour.

From this, it is clear that you have to slice the apples, butter the dish, pack the apples closely, and leave the dish uncovered. If you are going to bake it, it is clear that you have to put the dish in the oven, so you don't have to state that. Unlike a sentence delivered orally, this sentence can be re-read if the 'receiver' can't understand it. The information is packed as closely as the apples, without extraneous information and redundancies. This is what we mean by 'concise' and this is preferred in scientific writing. Similarly, scientists would not write:

- We designed a questionnaire.
- We asked participants to complete the questionnaire.

- A research assistant administered the questionnaire.

- We obtained the data.

They would pack all four facts closely by saying:

- Data were obtained by asking [participants] to complete an author-designed questionnaire administered by a research assistant (O'Neil, Lancee, & Freeman, 1985).

Obviously, there is a continuum in information-density. The more distant the audience is from you in knowledge, the more information has to be broken down and explained. In addition, there are times when you want to pack information loosely because you want to emphasize certain points.

As we go over various bits of text together, you can decide for yourself when the writing is too dense or too porous. Writing that is too dense packs so much information in one sentence that you cannot remember it immediately after reading it. If you have to re-read it, it is too dense. In overly-dense writing the emphasis is lost in the crowd. In contrast, 'porous' writing is like soup that has been watered down; it is too weak and loses its flavor. Secondly, porous writing takes up precious room when your article must conform to space limitations.

I admit that I am not writing this part and most of the book concisely because this is *not* a scientific text, as I define it. It is a *teaching* text, directed toward an audience whose native language is not English and who are novice writers. I feel more comfortable in a conversational tone because I have gained my experience through teaching. I am not presenting facts here but guiding people through a process; in that case, the writing should be reader friendly.

Guidelines for Conciseness

1. Some information isn't necessary to state at all. You can omit actions that are a necessary part of other actions: *After addressing the envelopes, we mailed the questionnaires to the respondents. Mailed* includes *addressing the envelopes.* If the whole context were known, we might even see that it was obvious that the questionnaires were mailed and not handed to the respondents. Obviously, in another context, you might have reason to stress that these questionnaires went through the mail (and some were therefore lost).

   Similarly, it is redundant to say: *Jones studied drug addiction and found that it …* since *found* includes *studied.*

2. Some words supply no information and merely take up space, such as the following words in italics:

   - The Middle East is *an area that is located geographically* northeast of Africa.

Although the list of such redundancies is long, I will single out only three examples:

- A current bete-noir is: This *period of time* (Instead of *this time* or *this period*)

- I have *formulated the hypothesis* that .... (Instead of: *I hypothesize that* ....)

- We will be able to *make estimations* of .... (Instead of: *We will be able to estimate*)

3. Sometimes a long phrase can be replaced by an appropriate conjunction:

- [Author lists reasons] This fact seems very important, especially for women, because *of the reasons already mentioned*.

- Rewritten: [Author lists reasons.] '*Therefore*, this fact seems very important, especially for women' where *Therefore* signals that the sentence is a conclusion drawn from previous reasons.

4. Sometimes changing the structure of the sentence can eliminate unwieldy phrases. In the following sentence we made two changes.

- Only after a long period (a) in which we updated the objectives (b) according to the remarks made by the readers we mentioned, we could come to the next stage ....

Part (a) can be expressed more concisely by changing a complete clause— *we updated the objectives*—into a simple gerund (a noun expressing an activity) i.e., *updating*.

Part (b) *the remarks made by the readers we mentioned*. If you say *the readers*, it is clear that you have already mentioned them. *The remarks made by the readers* is a long way of saying *the readers' remarks*. The same information in more concise form is:

- *We could come to the next stage only after a long period of updating the objectives according to the readers' remarks.*

5. Sometimes making the sentence more concise makes it more emphatic. Compare the student's version (a) and the revised version (b):

a. *The process of local government privatization did not begin as a result of planning.*

b. *The beginning of the process of local government privatization was not planned.*

Suppose you want to combine sentences, but not lose any information. The passive form can be the basis for adjectives, through the following process:

1. *We interviewed people from XYZ. They make up a sample that is representative of the population.*

Change to passive:

- *The people were interviewed.*

Insert the next information into a clause beginning with the appropriate relative pronoun (*who, which,* or *that*). Combine the two sentences, giving us:

- *The people who were **interviewed** make up a sample that is representative of the population.*

The relative pronoun and verb *to be* can be deleted so that we get:

- *The people interviewed make up a sample [that is] representative of the population.*

Interviewed now becomes an adjective describing the people; the main verb is now *make up.* But be aware that this compression also changes the balance of information so that *interviewed* is now secondary order information and *make up a sample* is primary.

2. *We obtained data from the 2000 census. These data proved to be inaccurate.*

   a. Passive form: *Data were obtained ....*

   b. Combining: *Data from the 2000 census were obtained, which proved to be inaccurate.*

   c. Deletion: *Data obtained from the 2000 census ....*

   Data obtained from the 2000 census proved to be inaccurate.

Task:

For practice, rewrite the following sentences more concisely, but be careful not to omit any information. In most cases, in addition to deleting words, some rewriting will be necessary to make the sentences more concise. Unfortunately, there isn't room here to provide the context, which is certainly relevant to your revision. However, most of the sentences were written as part of students' discussion of their research, while sentences 4 and 8 were responses to the question, 'What should the government do to improve the environment or the health of its citizens?'

Example:

Original sentence:

- *My study will take place in a hospital and I will study stress and the effects of stress on hospital patients.*

I rewrote the sentence assuming the statement conforms to our usual expectations. In that case, the usual place to study patients is in the hospital, so that the first part of the sentence is redundant. If the author wanted to meet patients in their homes, she would have to state that. Also, the author will probably not study stress itself, but only the effects of stress. Therefore, she could have stated it more concisely as:

- *My study will be on the effects of stress on hospital patients.*

To fine tune this to academic register, we might say:

- *My study will <u>focus on</u> the effects of stress on hospital patients.*

Now rewrite the following sentences to make them more concise.

1. My research thesis is named "Life in the Future." It is concerned with ….

2. [Author tells what she has done already.] The next stage of testing, that is yet to take place, will be comparing populations.

3. Before dealing with the main debates in my research area, I will try to summarize the current field briefly in a scientific way.

4. If the place you live in gives you the opportunity to throw out the trash by its type for recycling process, use this service.

5. Cohen does not agree with the explanation of Smith et al. because this hypothesis does not explain several important facts.

6. The purpose of the therapeutic process is to reintegrate the patients into their natural environment. This purpose is accomplished by proposing an integrative treatment that joins together medication and psychosocial rehabilitative treatment.

7. The purpose of the research is to study the subject of the well being of elderly who are residents in old age homes and the way it's influenced by 3 categories of variables.

8. In order to find a cure for AIDS, the government should put aside funds and resources for that cause and encourage scientists to work on it. In order to prevent the disease from spreading, children should be educated about AIDS in schools. They should be educated about how one can be infected and how to avoid it. With the proper education and with massive research on the HIV virus there is a chance for a healthier society.

Discussion

Below, I present each problem and a possible solution. Your solution may be perfectly acceptable, as long as you succeeded in deleting redundancies while preserving all the information.

1. My research thesis is named Life in the Future. It is concerned with ....

    First of all, *research thesis* is redundant. Secondly, I think the author meant to tell us the topic, not the title, of her research. In any case, a title or name is presented thusly:

    - In my thesis, "Life in the Future", I present the results of research on ...

    or she can say:

    - My thesis, "Life in the Future", is concerned with ....

2. The next stage of testing, that is yet to take place, will be comparing populations.

    'Next' includes *'that is yet to take place'* so the second phrase is redundant.

3. Before dealing with the main debates in my research area, I will try to summarize the current field briefly in a scientific way.

    The phrase *in a scientific way* is unnecessary; how else will he do it?

4. If the place you live in gives you the opportunity to throw out the trash by its type for recycling process, use this service.

    If the place you live in gives you the opportunity can be reduced to *if available (in your area)*

    to throw out the trash by its type for recycling process is all included in the verb *recycle*, which means precisely that

    use this service can be compressed. The final product depends upon who is giving you this order. The city council would probably say:

    - "Please use recycling facilities, if available in your area" or even "Recycle trash where possible".

5. Cohen does not agree with the explanation of Smith et al. because this hypothesis does not explain several important facts.

    Explanation, hypothesis, and *explain* are repetitive.

    Select a verb that is more specific; for example, *contends* includes *does not agree* but also allows you to add a clause stating why Cohen does not agree, as in:

    - Cohen contends that Smith et al.'s hypothesis does not explain (or *overlooks*) several important facts [or name the facts].

6. The purpose of the therapeutic process is to reintegrate the patients into their natural environment. This purpose is accomplished by

proposing an integrative treatment that joins together medication and psychosocial rehabilitative treatment.

This purpose is accomplished by proposing is redundant.

Integrative and *joins together* are repetitive.

We don't want to repeat the word *treatment*.

A possible revision:

- The purpose of the therapeutic process is to reintegrate the patients into their natural environment by treatment that integrates medication and psychosocial rehabilitative processes.

7. The purpose of the research is to study the subject of the well being of elderly who are residents in old age homes and the way it's influenced by 3 categories of variables.

elderly who are residents in old age homes is redundant because residents of old age homes **are** elderly

As in the example about the patients, given above, I doubt that the author is going to study well-being **and** the way it's influenced by ….

Possible revision:

- The purpose of the research is to study the influence of three categories of variables on the well-being of residents of old age homes.

8. There are two main ways to deal with the problem of AIDS. Firstly, in order to find a cure for AIDS, the government should put aside funds and resources for that cause and encourage scientists to work on it. Secondly, in order to prevent the disease from spreading, children should be educated about AIDS in schools. They should be educated about how one can be infected and how to avoid it. With the proper education and with massive research on the HIV virus there is a chance for a healthier society.

There's a lot of repetition here. For one thing *should put aside funds and resources for that cause* [and probably *and encourage scientists to work on it*] is included in *support research*. Maybe some more specific ways of supporting research can be added instead of the repetitions.

I leave you to write one sentence describing exactly what the goal in education about AIDS should be.

Chapter 6

Making Connections— Connectives

What Is the Role of Connectives?

Connectives are the words or phrases that bind together parts of a text. In order to appreciate connectives, let's look at a text without them, produced by a student (who has since learned about connectives and been promoted to Professor):

> Allen (1976) stated that ideology is only one component of the public belief system. Smith (1980) criticized the validity of one-dimensional ideological tags. They are rhetorical and do not reflect real political life. Cramer (1970) shows that interviewees are not always consistent about their belief systems ....

[followed by 10 references in this form, without any connections between them].

A text without connectives reads like a grocery list. What's more important, you cannot understand the point the author is trying to make.

There are many systems in a text that connect ideas and sentences. One is the system of pronouns, Chapter 2, Nouns and Pronouns. Other systems are discussed below.

Local Connectives (Between Two Clauses)

Let's talk first about local connectives—between two ideas or facts. An author can state two facts:

- Mary was not promoted. Her father is the Dean.

The reader doesn't know the connection between them unless the author tells us. The reader can think:

1. Mary was not promoted   *because*   her father is the Dean
2. Mary was not promoted   *although*   her father is the Dean.

We refer to words such as *because* and *although* as "logical connectors".

Now, I grant that most of the time, you can infer the logical connection between statements, but very often lack of connectives makes it difficult if not impossible to understand the author's point.

The following is from a published research text from which I have deleted the logical connectives.

> The majority of respondents showed improvement from the first to second interview, (1) _____ a sizable minority (27% to 37%) continued to experience a variety of symptoms .... (2) _____, the authors [Jones, Smith, and Brown] concluded from their data that bereavement is a relatively mild reaction for most subjects. (3) A thorough review of the research in this area, (3) _____, does not substantiate this view of the grieving process. (adapted from Lehman, Wortman, & Williams, 1987)

When the connectives are added, we can see that the authors feel very strongly that Jones, Smith, and Brown drew unreasonable conclusions from their study. If the authors had used *therefore* instead of *nonetheless* at the beginning of the second sentence, it would imply that J, S & B had reached a logical conclusion.

> The majority of respondents showed improvement from the first to second interview, <u>although</u> a sizable minority (27% to 37%) continued to experience a variety of symptoms .... <u>Nonetheless</u>, the authors [Jones, Smith, and Brown] concluded from their data that bereavement is a relatively mild reaction for most subjects.

> A thorough review of the research in this area, <u>however,</u> does not substantiate this view of the grieving process (Lehman et al. 1987: 218).

Global Connectives

We also need to tie larger chunks of the discourse together. Using global connectives, an author can signal the structure of the text. One way is to give a blueprint of what is to come and then to tell the readers where they are in that blueprint. Although a social scientist might not use these exact words, the blueprint method is common to all academic fields. For instance:

> So, it will be necessary to peel through <u>several layers of misunder-standing</u> before getting to those who not only understood what I was trying to say but appreciated the spirit in which I said it.

> The <u>first and most common misunderstanding</u> has been .... [followed by 9 paragraphs] For historicists, there are <u>two ways out</u> of this conundrum. <u>The first</u> is the path chosen by Hegel .... <u>The other path</u> was the one chosen by Nietzche and his twentieth-century followers like Heidegger ....

The second layer of misunderstanding of my article has to do with ….
(Fukuyama, 1989/90: 21–23)

Notice in the example above the clear boundaries between the first misunderstanding and the second misunderstanding. And between the 'two ways out', showing where Hegel ends and Nietzche begins. Such 'blueprints' make the text much more reader-friendly.

What Connectives Do We Use in Scientific Writing?

You can increase your vocabulary of connectives by the following exercise. Below I've given groups of local connectives and two groups of global connectives, (13 and 14), and your task is to provide the name of the category for each group. Use a word that will help you understand the function of this category. It doesn't have to be the "official" name. For example, look at the following group of words in italics:

- *Although/Even though/Though* it was raining, we went on the picnic.

  In spite of/Despite/Notwithstanding the rain, we went on the picnic.

  In spite of the fact that it was raining ….

The function of the words in italics above is to connect two statements, one that is "expected" or agreed upon, and one that is contrary to expectations. The official name for this group of connectives is **concession** but you can think of it as a form of **contradiction**. As I showed in Chapter 1, Rhetoric, the placement of the connective changes the emphasis:

- although the sample was small, the results were significant.
- although the results were significant, the sample was small.

By using the apppropriate connectives, you can signal the "expected" clause:

- *Although/Even though/Though* it was raining, we went on the picnic.

or the clause that is contrary to expectations:

- It was raining; *however,* /*but/nevertheless/yet/nonetheless*, we went on the picnic.

The following connectives also signal the expected clause, but they must be followed by a noun or noun phrase:

- *in spite of* [+NOUN]/*notwithstanding* [+NOUN]/*despite* [+NOUN]
- *In spite of/Notwithstanding/Despite* the rain, we went on the picnic …
- *In spite of the fact* that it was raining …

The terms in this example can be categorized as follows:

Local Connectives

1. To signal concession

    a. to signal the 'expected' clause

        i. these signals take a noun phrase

            - *in spite of* [+NOUN]/*notwithstanding* [+NOUN]/*despite* [+NOUN]

        ii. these signals take a clause

            - Although/Even though/Though

    b. to signal the clause that is contrary to expectations

        - *however, /but* [no comma]/*nevertheless, /yet, /nonetheless*

Fill in the name of each category and subcategory. Use your own terms or if you prefer, use the labels from the Functions of Categories below.

2. Name of category _____

    a. *While/Whereas* his solution is theoretical, hers is more practical.

    In contrast to sociology, anthropology deals with particular groups.

    Sociology deals with society in general; *however/but* anthropology deals with particular groups

    Name of subcategory _____

    b. *On the one hand*, high tech pays very well. *On the other hand*, you have to work long hours.

    Name of subcategory _____

3. _____

    If the action (*we leave now*) is carried out:

    - We will catch the bus, *provided that/if* we leave now.

    IF the action is not carried out:

    - We'd better leave now; *otherwise,* (i.e., if we don't leave now) we will miss the bus.

    - We will miss the bus, *unless* we leave now (i.e., if we don't leave now).

4. _____

    - *Likewise,*

    - *Similarly,*

5. _____

- *Because/Since* connectives are very important, I am giving you this list.
- *as a result of* [+NOUN]
- *due to* [+NOUN]
- *on account of* [+NOUN]
- *As a result of/Due to/On account of/*the budget cuts, we have to fire staff.
- *as*—The store was closed on Tuesday, *as* it was a holiday.

6. _____

- This is not a good solution. *As a matter of fact, /In fact, /Indeed, /On the contrary*, it can cause a lot of harm.
- People are not reading books anymore. *Rather, [Instead]*, they are getting most of their information from the internet.

7. _____

- She is a linguist, *i.e., /in other words/ namely*, a person who studies the theory of language.

8. _____

All members of the group are named:

- I am going to three countries, *namely, /specifically*, France, England, and Holland.

One or more members of the group are singled out:

- There are many museums I like to visit, *in particular*, the Louvre.

9. _____

- *e.g.,*
- *for instance,*
- *such as*

10. _____

- I missed the bus. *Therefore, /Hence, /Thus, /Consequently, /As a consequence, /As a result, /So*, I missed an important lecture.
- Many people don't read English. *Accordingly*, all the signs in the terminal are in several languages.
- Use a spell checker. *Then* you won't make so many mistakes.

11. _____

Both alternatives are open:

- Two theories are investigated here. The X hypothesis is based on …. *Alternatively*, the Y hypothesis states that ….

12. _____

- *In order to* get the results more quickly, we contacted people by e-mail.

- We contacted people by e-mail *so that* we would get the results more quickly.

Global Connectives

13. _____

a. at the beginning of the text:

- *Briefly,*

b. at the end of the text:

- *In short,*

- *In conclusion,*

- *To sum up,*

14. _____

Let's say you want to tie different parts of your text together. For example, your opening sentence is:

- There are many reasons that knowing English is important.

To mark the beginning:

- *To begin with, /Firstly,* it has become the common language of the internet.

To add statements:

- *In addition, /Also, /Besides, /Furthermore, /Moreover,* English is the predominant language in scientific journals.

To mark the end:

- *Finally, /Lastly,* it is much easier to learn than Chinese.

Functions of Categories

To signal a contrast between two entities

To signal a contrast between two aspects of the same entity

To signal a consequence, result, effect

To signal an example

To signal a cause, reason

To state things in other words

To signal a purpose

To signal similarity

To mark boundaries between subunits of a general statement

To reinforce a statement

To show two equally preferred options

To signal a condition (See also Chapter 3, Verbs, Conditional Sentences)

To signal a summary

To itemize

To show contrast

Until now, I've listed connectives for formal, written discourse. However, when you give a talk, it is acceptable to use a slightly less formal, or even colloquial, register. During your talk, you might find the following connectors helpful:

To depart from the topic:

- *Incidentally,*
- *By the way,*

To return to the topic:

- *At any rate,*
- *In any event/case,*

As in:

> There are many important social problems in the world today. *Incidentally*, a cure for cancer has just been found. *In any event*, the problems concerning human aggression have not been solved.

To be more exact:

- *Actually,*

- I've just written a book. *Actually*, I had 6 co-authors ....

To offer an explanation:

- *After all,*

- Poor people usually do not receive higher education. *After all*, how can they afford tuition of $20,000 a year?

To save face of your audience:

- *needless to say, obviously, of course, as we know, admittedly*

Although I've heard people argue, "If it's *needless*, why say it?", I find expressions such as the above useful in stating something simple without sounding patronizing. These expressions acknowledge that your audience probably knows the statement to follow, but it gives you a chance to slip it in, in case they don't. Furthermore, these expressions also can signal that you're conceding a point, e.g., *Admittedly*, I have taken many liberties with the names of these categories, but I want to keep things simple.

Concession:

I know everyone wants to go out to lunch; *still*, I must finish my talk.

Chapter 7

Understanding Genre Analysis—Introductions

As I discussed in Chapter 1, scientific texts belong to different genres, of which a research report is one. You could say the *sine qua non* of an empirical research article is the following structure: introduction, methods, results, and discussion. The introduction to a research report can be called a *sub-genre* because it has to conform to expected genre structures. Chapter 1 presents a passage about nonsense, which *sounds* like authentic research because it is written in the appropriate structure of a research report. Conversely, authentic research will *not* sound like a research report if it does not conform to the expected structure. If you want to write successful Introductions, you first need to know what the genre requires. In this chapter, I go into more detail about the meaning of genre. First, let's compare two versions of an Introduction, one that was published and one that I rewrote. The original text was chosen because it conforms to the genre structure even though it is extremely brief.[1] Which do you recognize as the authentic introduction?

Text A

Who has not, during a time of illness or pain, cried out to a higher being for help and healing? Praying for help and healing is a fundamental concept in practically all societies, though the object to which these prayers are directed varies among the religions of the world. In western culture, the idea of praying for the benefit of others (intercessory prayer) to … God is widely accepted and practiced. However, the medical literature contains no scientific evidence either confirming or negating the healing effectiveness of intercessory prayer. In only a few studies have scientific methods been used to attempt to determine whether or not prayer is therapeutically effective and these studies have been inconclusive.

My study concerning prayer and patients in a general hospital coronary care unit was designed to answer two questions:

(1) Does intercessory prayer to … God have any effect on the patient's medical condition and recovery while in the hospital? (2) How are these effects characterized, if present?

Text B

Who has not, during a time of illness or pain, cried out to a higher being for help and healing? Praying for help and healing is a fundamental concept in practically all societies, though the object to which these prayers are directed varies among the religions of the world. Although in western culture, the idea of praying for the benefit of others (intercessory prayer) to ... God is widely accepted and practiced among the general population, it is not given enough attention by medical personnel as an alternative or even supplementary method. Moreover, doctors sometimes discourage prayer among patients, believing that it will give them false hopes. We believe prayer by patients should be encouraged and a system of intercessory prayer should be established by hospitals for their patients.

The benefits of prayer are many, such as ....

You undoubtedly chose **Text A** (Byrd, 1988: 826) as the authentic text because it conformed to your mental representation of the structure of an introduction to a research article. This expected structure that you have absorbed after reading many published articles represents the *genre*. **Text B**, which is about the same subject, seems to be the opening to an opinion essay or even an editorial advocating prayer.

In discourse analysis, *genre* is defined differently from other fields[2]. In this view, scientific writing consists of many genres, such as theses, proposals, letters, reviews, and grant requests. Although scientific texts may share certain structures, no one pattern fits them all; that is why "scientific writing" is not a genre but consists of many genres. For instance, in a talk at a conference, in contrast to a journal article, it is appropriate to include greetings to the audience, perhaps even a personal anecdote or joke, almost no reference to previous literature, and a summary. Genre is also not defined by content; although both texts above were about prayer, they represented different genres because they did not have a common purpose. A conversation is not a genre but a warning conversation between a parent and a child is. A letter *per se* is not a genre, but a job application letter is one genre and a sales pitch letter is another, although they both share openings and closings (*Dear Mr. X; Sincerely*).

Although we are discussing *genre* in scientific texts, you could say all of social life consists of going from one genre to another—from the class meeting, lecture, seminar, or conference to the dinner with family or cocktail party. Genres are composed of verbal structures, usually in a prescribed order, recognized by particular social groups. When some structures are not realized or the order is changed, we often experience cultural dissonance. When I visited Australia, I did not understand that 'payment' in a restaurant, at least the ones I went to, came before 'meal'. Academic genres, in contrast, often are shared by people across national and ethnic boundaries. Swales (1990) refers to scientists as a type of 'discourse community'. We can define 'community' as people who agree upon the conventions of discourse. The following authors are very explicit:

> Genres are the media through which scholars and scientists communicate with their peers. Genres are intimately linked to a discipline's methodology and they package information in ways that conform to a discipline's norms, values, and ideology. Understanding the genres of written communication in one's field is, therefore, essential to professional success (Berkenkotter & Huckin, 1995: 1).

What Are the Expected Structures in Introductions?

It would be nearly impossible to have examples of every genre you might encounter in your professional life. However, you can learn to analyze new genres and model your writing according to them. How do we analyze genre? We look through several typical texts and try to find the common rhetorical purposes in each segment. For instance, looking at **Text A**, above, I find it easily falls into three segments, according to rhetorical purpose:

1. Who has not, during a time of illness or pain, cried out to a higher being for help and healing? Praying for help and healing is a fundamental concept in practically all societies ….

2. However the medical literature contains no scientific evidence either confirming or negating the healing effectiveness of intercessory prayer. In only a few studies have scientific methods been used to attempt to determine whether or not prayer is therapeutically effective and these studies have been inconclusive.

3. My study concerning prayer and patients in a general hospital coronary care unit was designed to answer two questions: ….

When we define a segment by its purpose, we call it a 'move'.

In Move 1, the authors justify their choice of phenomena for intensive study by appealing to its significance, importance, or worthwhileness. I call this Move *establishing relevance*.

In Move 2, the authors point out that the knowledge about the phenomena that they have chosen is incomplete. To borrow Swales' (1990) ecological metaphor, the authors seek some no-man's land upon which to set up stakes; I label this move *establishing the gap the present research is meant to fill*.

Lastly, in Move 3, which I term *previewing the authors' contribution*, they declare that they have taken possession. In this genre, the declaration entails the promise that the account of this investigation represents the contents of the article to follow. If even two of these moves are present, you recognize the text as an Introduction, even if the content is nonsense, as illustrated by the satirical piece about childhood, in Chapter 1. When we speak about typical structures of a particular genre, it is analogous to saying that the 'typical' components of a dinner are: soup, salad, main course, dessert, tea or coffee. We would recognize the meal served as 'dinner' if only one of the first 3 courses were served; dessert and a hot beverage are usual but not obligatory.

Below are examples of moves from introductions in various fields and journals. For the sake of brevity, I have tried to present examples consisting of one sentence but it should be kept in mind that a move may be accomplished in any length of text, from one clause to many paragraphs; see the varying lengths of moves in Text A. Furthermore, the three moves might be repeated for each variable in the study, creating more than one instance of a certain move in each introduction.

Establishing Relevance

What is 'relevant' is admittedly relative but we need to show that the phenomenon under study is worthy of study. Relevance is usually established by describing the phenomenon as important, significant, or salient. The following example seems to incorporate all these traits: (Since the relevance claim may be a reflection of the journal audience, I've included the source in each example. I have also italicized the expressions of relevance.)

> Scandals are *ubiquitous* social phenomena with *unique salience* and singular *dramatic intensity*. [Author then explains their social consequences] (Adut, 2005, *American Journal of Sociology*).

In addition, we find that Move 1 is framed as relevant for one of two areas, probably reflecting the perspective of the journal in either theoretical or applied research. The research can be intrinsically relevant, which in effect is a rather tautological claim that 'the research is important because it is mainstream' as in:

> To investigate filtering mechanisms in selective attention, *a great deal of effort has been put* toward investigating the processing of irrelevant information (Lammertyn & Fias, 2005, *Quarterly Journal of Experimental Psychology*).

or relevant because of its implications to society, or for human welfare as in:

> Adolescent depression is important .... Elucidation of which *nonshared environmental influences are important in the etiology of adolescent depression* would be of great interest and is the focus for our study (Liang & Eley, 2005, *Child Development*).

If it is directed toward research, the move includes an expression to show the magnitude of this research by referring to the number of publications (*many investigators, growing interest, much attention*) or the length of time the phenomenon has been studied.

It is possible, of course, to address the claim to both worlds, as in the following extract, which claims the research is necessary for *scholarly* (i.e., theoretical) and *policy* (i.e., applied) levels:

> With the advent of interest in so-called 'supply-side' economics, the effects of taxation on aggregate economic activity and economic growth have become important issues at both the scholarly and policy levels (Koester & Kormendi, 1989, *Economic Inquiry*).

If the relevance is directed toward the social importance of the phenomenon, it can be presented either as a growing phenomenon (1) or, in contrast, an eternal phenomenon (2):

1. For not only did the volume and rate of nonagricultural self-employment stabilize in the 1950's, they *have been declining* once again since 1983 (Linder & Houghton, 1990: 727, *American Journal of Sociology*).

2. Praying for help and healing is a fundamental concept in practically all societies … (Byrd, 1988: 826).

The question remains of how to frame the phenomenon. The following openings appear in two papers in *Child Development*, both comparing the achievements of Asian and U.S. children. Interestingly, the emphasis of each group of authors is quite different:

1. Cross national studies have shown that by first grade, the mathematics achievement of school-age children in the US lags behind that of children in Asian countries such as Japan and Taiwan (Song & Ginsburg, 1987: 1286).

2. It has been obvious for some time that Asian students far out-perform their American counterparts in mathematics and science (Stigler, Lee & Stevenson, 1987: 1272).

Level of Generality

Move 1 starts with the general field, e.g., *Scandals are ubiquitous social phenomena*, (above) and narrows it down to the specific focus of the present research, the scandal surrounding Oscar Wilde in Victorian England. The focus is further refined in the following two moves.

Establishing the Gap

We now have to show that our research is not only relevant but provides a missing piece of information about the phenomenon. This move is often signaled by a connector such as *although* or *however* that indicates that the text is going to change direction from the known to the unknown (e.g., *However, the medical literature contains no scientific evidence* … in the 'prayer' text above).

Unlike Moves 1 and 3, Move 2 can tread on the toes of other citizens of academia. Therefore, the wording is especially important. The most neutral claim is: *There is a scarcity of research in the field.* This claim has a more or less standard form, but variations depending on which grammatical subject is chosen; see Chapter 2 on count and uncount nouns. For instance:

- **Uncount nouns:**

  Little research/attention has been focused on X; there has been *much* research on X, *less* on Y

- **Count nouns:**

  There have been *few* studies on Y; *many* studies on X, *fewer* on Y

- **Both count and uncount:**

  Research/literature on X is *rare, scarce* or *limited*

  Investigations of X are *rare, scarce* or *limited*

- **Focusing on the phenomenon:**

  The role of X has been largely *unexamined/neglected/overlooked.*

This kind of claim is not based on actual numbers. In fact, it can be made even if literature has been cited. Although this kind of claim is not contentious, authors sometimes take the additional step of acknowledging that they may be mistaken, as in: '*To our knowledge*, no studies have examined ….' As a student remarked, you can never be sure you have checked *all* the data bases. In fact, I came across one example in which the authors try to anticipate exactly that issue:

> Of the nearly 1,200 published studies to date with the terms marital separation or divorce in their titles, we know of only four prospective longitudinal studies that have attempted to predict future separation and divorce [citations] (Gottman & Leveson, 1992: 221).

Another kind of claim acknowledges that research has been done, but it has not sufficiently solved the problem, i.e., the answer is still obscure. A claim of *obscurity* can be made without mentioning any particular individual, by making the criticism general, as in

- However, the findings of these [mentioned] studies were generally inconclusive.

- [In spite of these studies] the exact factors responsible for X remain undetermined/unknown/unclear.

When we point out specific *defects* in previous research, we enter more risky territory. However, again, the criticism can be generalized:

- Previous studies are limited/inaccurate/fail to do X/have not done X/

- A concern/problem/shortcoming in previous studies is …

- Many previous studies on [X] have not included control or comparison groups (Lehman, Wortman, & Williams, 1987: 219, *J of Personality and Social Psychology*).

The territory becomes more treacherous when we claim defects in a particular person or study, as in these examples:

(1) The major problem with Marsden's study is that his choice of countries to be paired seems essentially ad hoc, and for this reason alone a more systematic approach is warranted (Koester & Kormendi, 1989, *Economic Inquiry*).

(2) the inaccurate scale of degrees of certainty provided in Cooper [Ref.] … suggests she has never consulted a reference text on [linguistic topic] (Holmes, 1988).

(3) I develop a new measure of product diversity and use it to present evidence that contradicts one of [previous author's] primary results (Alexander, 1996).

In (1) criticism is leveled at the person's work (*Marsden's study, his choice of countries*) rather than the person himself, unlike in (2), which implies a defect in the person (*she has never consulted …*) (Lewin, 2005b). Holmes might have aimed her criticism at Cooper's scale of degrees of certainty rather than at Cooper herself, perhaps by explaining why she takes issue with some of the points in the scale. Notice also that the criticism in (1) is mitigated by introducing uncertainty (*seems essentially*) while Holmes in (2) (*has never*) and Alexander in (3) (*contradicts*) make claims that leave no room for doubt. For strategies to soften criticism, see the section on *hedging* in Chapter 11, Discussions. Another way to mitigate criticism is to begin with a compliment e.g., *X's path-breaking work*. Unfortunately, authors so rarely compliment one another that, if they do, the reader is apt to suspect that a criticism will follow.

In sum, if, in your field, it is customary to establish the gap, pay attention to the prevailing norms as to how it is done. It does seem that certain fields tend to make general criticisms, while others seem to feel that they must weaken arguments of particular people in order to make their claims. If in your field, it is necessary to stress the defects in particular pieces of research, try to mitigate the criticism.

Previewing the Author's Contribution

Until this point in the Introduction, a certain amount of tension has been building up. A particular intellectual area has been defined in Move 1 and a gap within this area has been located in Move 2. In Move 3, the authors declare that they have carried out an investigation to close this gap. In fact, in many instances, they state indirectly that they have closed the gap. This move has two main directions; either the authors describe the purpose of the study, as in (a) and (b), below, and leave us in suspense as to the results or they preview the contents of the article, as in (c), and reveal the results of the study.

a. The initial aims of this study were to determine the extent .... We also examine the longer-term complications associated with the emergent symptom clusters (Prigerson et al., 1995, *American Journal of Psychiatry*).

Below, (b) and (c) are from *J of Experimental Psychology: Learning, Memory and Cognition*:

b. The purpose of this study is twofold: (i) to identify determinants of word translation ... (ii) to explore different versions of the translation task (de Groot, 1992).

c. Four experiments are presented in which the numerical distance between prime distractor and probe target was manipulated. [describes experiment, results of Experiment 1] in Experiment 2, similar results were obtained .... Experiment 3 showed that these observations also hold for numbers presented verbally .... (Experiment 4) revealed no NP whatsoever ... (Schwartz & Metcalfe, 1992).

In contrast to the previous moves, the beginning of Move 3 is always signaled, by a reference to the authors (as the agents), their research (*this study, the present work*) or the publication itself (*here*). The rhetorical impact is heightened by the fact that if authors have used the passive voice to describe previous literature, they introduce their own work in the active voice (*we report here, we examine*). (See Chapter 3, Verbs, section on passive.) As you will learn from the section on hedging in Chapter 11, some scientists find it prudent to tone down (i.e., hedge) their accomplishments, introducing Move 3 with phrases such as: in this study, we *begin to examine* ..., this study is *a preliminary effort* at providing an ... examination.

Outlining the Contents

In especially long articles, such as in economics, an additional move is sometimes necessary in which the author details the contents of each section:

> Section 1 develops the model. Section II gives the conditions for debt neutrality .... Section III illustrates the different effects of changes ... (Buiter, 1988, *The Economic Journal*).

In a variation on Moves 1, 2, and 3 as presented above, the gap is not represented as missing information that must be supplied but as mistaken ideas that must be corrected. In this variation, Move 1 states the prevailing view, Move 2 posits an alternative view and Move 3 states how the article will explain or prove the alternative view, as in the following three examples of introductions:

1. **The politics of the web: the case of one newsgroup**

    Move 1: What does it mean that the internet ... is political? [Cites view that there can be no politics of the internet since everyone has equal access to it.]

Move 2: Despite this popular line of reasoning, I would argue that one should consider not only the politics *on* the web but also the politics *of* the web [italics in the original].

Move 3: In what follows, I argue that rivalries on the net are structured by …. I will justify these points by … (Waldstein, 2005).

In the next example, the preview (Move 3) is presented before the gap (Move 2).

2. **Is political conservatism synonymous with authoritarianism?**

Move 1: Rightists are authoritarian … and generally rigid in their approach to dealing with social information—that is a common assumption among lay persons on the political left [citation]

Move 3: An important assumption of the present result is that the adoption of politically conservative attitudes may not necessarily indicate in the adoptee any mental rigidity ….

Move 2: Rather, specific types of conservative attitudes may be differentiated on the basis of their distinct relationships with content free … cognitive motivation … (Crowson, Thoma, & Hestevold, 2005).

3. **Five approaches to explaining 'truth' and 'deception' in human communication**

Move 1: In the social sciences, explanations are usually presented as answers to questions.

Move 2: But in fieldwork-infused fields like anthropology, sometimes questions are not deliberate, science-like deductions from theories but rather are inductively inspired ….

Move 3: This article traces my understanding of one problem by identifying five frames through which I have attempted to understand this topic (Blum, 2005).

Review of Literature

I have not labeled 'review of literature' as a move, although it is a necessary feature of an introduction. This is because literature references can support Move 1, 2 or 3, or all of them or, even appear as a separate section after the Introduction, as in a Ph.D. dissertation. Chapter 8 is devoted to the review of literature.

Order

Although Moves 1, 2, and 3 usually appear in linear order, there may be deviations, such as Move 3 appearing first. Also, if there is more than one variable to be presented, the authors may choose to discuss each in turn, as in this created text:

- An area of major concern in some communities is the poor reading performance of schoolchildren ...

   ### Variable I

   Move 1: Much attention has been focused on the role of neurological deficits ....

   Move 2: However, no research has determined the effect of schooling on these deficits.

   ### Variable II

   Move 1: An almost equal emphasis has been placed on educational practices that may impede reading

   Move 2: In this research, classes of children were studied and no individual testing was done for neurological deficits.

   Move 3: We report here the results of two studies of the interaction of educational practices and neurological deficits.

Options vs. Context

The possibilities I have presented for each move are context-dependent, as are other examples throughout this book. The choices within the genre—whether one of the three moves is absent and which variations are chosen for each move—depend upon what is typical of your field, even of your tiny specialization within that field and of your target journal. For instance, in a very new field, it might not be necessary to 'establish a gap'. I would also think that who *you* are—student, well-known researcher, maverick in the field—would impinge upon the type of claim and the type of language you would use. In my view, genre is analogous to iambic pentameter and stanzas in poetry; against these constraints, an infinite number of poems can be written. In fact, even though the genre imposes a prescribed structure on texts, each text is unique rhetorically, i.e., the way it expounds its ideas.

Tasks: Analyzing Introductions

The way to learn is to study carefully how introductions (as well as other sections) are composed in your field and in your target journal (the one to which you would like to submit your paper).

1. Photocopy five introductions from your journal. Divide the introductions according to moves. Did you find Moves 1, 2, and 3? Did you find any additional moves? If so, what is their purpose?

2. What is the usual order of the moves?

3. What proportion of text is devoted to each move? For instance, is the emphasis on the background and establishing relevance or establishing the gap?

4. Write a mini-introduction to your proposed research. In two sentences each, explain the relevance, explain what is lacking in previous research, and tell what you propose to do for your study.

I have discussed the structure of the Introduction in this chapter. Now you need help with specifics such as grammar and style. Specifics are discussed in the following chapters:

A. Verbs: Chapter 3

B. Review of Literature: Chapter 8

C. Shaping Sentences: Chapter 4

Notes:

[1] We do not necessarily endorse any part of the content of this or any other example.

[2] For my understanding of genre, I am indebted to M.A.K. Halliday, J. Martin, and R. Hasan (see bibliography on genre), as well as to Swales (1990).

Chapter 8

Review of the Literature

Background

One of the necessary components of many scientific genres is the review of literature on the general topic under study. In journal articles, the review is a prominent part of the introduction, although individual references to previous literature are often found in the other sections as well. In a dissertation, the review of literature may occupy an entire chapter.

Within articles or dissertations, the importance of the review varies greatly. In some texts, the review of the literature <u>is</u> the essence of the work, as the author reinterprets or contests a dominant view or views. In others, prominence is on the authors' own work and previous literature is very much in the background. In the next sections, I discuss some basic characteristics that have been mentioned in the literature. Then I offer some guidelines for your own review.

What Constitutes a Reference to Literature?

The first question for potential writers in any field is, 'What constitutes a reference to literature?' In other words, when is a claim or fact part of general knowledge or consensus, and when does it have to be attributed to a specific author? One might think that there is a consensus about certain claims, such as 'Drug addiction is a growing problem around the world.' Remarkably, there is often support or justification (in the form of references to literature) for even the most uncontested claims such as:

> Marital dissolution is a serious social issue in terms of its negative consequences for the mental and physical health of spouses [Citations] and their children [Citations] (Gottman & Leveson, 1992).

In particular, social workers have informed me that there is no consensus about which social problems are most pressing and so they always try to give sources to strengthen their claims. A similar problem arises when theories are mentioned. Aren't some theories such as '*Our dreams show our unconscious thoughts*' so mainstream that they no longer need be name-tagged, so that (Freud, 19XX) would be superfluous? To resolve this problem, one should be guided by the convention in the field under study.

Giving Credit Where Credit Is Due

Needless to say, for every claim or finding that is <u>not</u> taken for granted in the field, due credit must be given by including the source (the name of the author and the details of publication). Findings and claims given in a paper or talk (whether published or unpublished) are the original author's intellectual property and must be treated as any other property. In the university setting, the authorities usually have the right to dismiss a student found guilty of plagiarism; in the wider community, the original authors can bring legal action against writers who 'borrow' their ideas without naming the source. Therefore, while you are composing, especially if you are downloading from an electronic data base, it is essential to keep track of the parts of the text that are exact quotes and also to copy the complete source.[1]

How Extensive Should the Review of Literature Be?

We would expect a difference across genres; in **a doctoral proposal or dissertation**, students have to show that they have a grasp of the wider field, as well as of the narrower area of their particular research; in **a research report for a journal**, the immediate background is necessary but how wide the coverage should be depends on the field. For example, sociology cited many more references than did physics, when articles from a given year (1997) were compared (Hyland, 1999). Within fields, some journals may have an audience that is so specialized one could assume all the readers are familiar with the basic texts in the field. For instance, the audience of *The Gerontologist* is more specialized than the audience of *Social Work*. In contrast to these written texts, **an oral presentation** at a meeting must concentrate on the author's own work as very little time is available for giving a broad overview of the field.

Why Do We Incorporate Other People's Ideas?

The motivations for including references to literature run the gamut from respect for previous scholars to self-enhancement. Citations are a way of saying 'Thank you' to people who've done a good job, to paraphrase Ravetz (1971, cited in Swales, 1990). To put it more strongly, citations are used 'to pay intellectual debts' (Dong, 1996: 429). The other reasons seem to tip the scale in favor of egoistical motivations. As Swales (1990) states, citations demonstrate that the writer is familiar with the field and qualifies as a member of the chosen scholarly community.

References also lay the groundwork for the writer's present research. Besides, each research text can be considered as a turn in a dialogue with other scientists. Each text responds to past texts and hopefully, will be the basis for response by others. Furthermore, citations show that we are aligning ourselves with current concerns in the field. References can go beyond relevance by providing a background against which our own position looks particularly innovative (Gilbert, 1976; Berkenhotter & Huckin, 1995, cited in Hyland, 1999).

The Psychological Force of References

The impact of references is not based only on rhetorical power. Some would say that references have psychological force in establishing credibility to our stance. Latané's theory of social impact states that:

> the impact of a source on a target individual is a function of the strength (e.g., expertise and credibility ... and number of sources) (Latané & Nida, 1980, cited in Shadish & Fuller, 1994: 52).

These findings fuel Latour's (1987) argument:

> that scholarly citations in an article serve this sort of function, increasing the number and strength of things that a critic has to attack to discredit an article (cited in Shadish & Fuller, 1994: 52).

Not only may references have a psychological impact on the ultimate audience, but they may play a part in influencing the gatekeepers of the target journal. In studies cited by Shadish and Fuller (1994), *review of the literature* was ranked by editors of two journals from 7–8 among 14–15 item sets of criteria used to judge the quality of research papers submitted to them for publication.

Criteria for Selecting References

In addition to the extent and quality of the review, there are selection criteria for who gets cited. Acknowledging that there are biases in coverage of the literature, Shadish and Fuller point out 'that the author of theoretically oriented research selectively cites work that bears positively on the theorizing' (Shadish & Fuller, 1994: 241). In addition, they claim, recency may be a criterion of selection. An analysis of two journals (the *Journal of Personality and Social Psychology* and the *Psychological Review*) demonstrates that 50% of citations fell within five years of the article's submission date.

To ideology and recency, I should add that political exigencies must be taken into account. Dissertation writers especially should remember to acknowledge prominent members of the field, especially those in their own geographical area, department, and so on, who might expect to be mentioned. Feelings of injury can run very deep, as the following quote from an omitted researcher reflects:

> It was my understanding that Lieberson and Bell know [my previous] works. Why did they not mention them? .... I first presented this idea, nearly in the same terms, in an article published 14 years ago (Besnard

1979). This article is not mentioned, although I assume that Lieberson knew it, for I sent it to him at his request in 1988 (Besnard, 1995).

Irrespective of whether you are justified in omitting someone's work, consider the possible repercussions.

References and Rhetorical Moves

Obviously, in Introductions, references bolster the rhetorical move of Establishing Relevance (see Chapter 7) as shown above in '*Marital dissolution is a serious social issue ....*' References can support other moves as well. The author can even support a claim of 'research is scarce', i.e., establish the gap, by citing previous literature, as in:

> Despite the large number of private justice systems and the even larger number of private police who operate and maintain them, *little is known about the factors that shape private corporate justice (Marx 1987: 188)*. Sociologists have ignored private justice and private police in favor of [the] study of public justice and public police [citations] (Davis, Lundman, & Martinez, 1991) [emphasis added].

Instead of a review of all the relevant literature, the Discussion (or Conclusion) usually calls for some comparison of present findings and explanations (hopefully in the form of corroboration) to previous literature as in:

> Finally, there are important links between private corporate justice and public criminal justice. Shearing and Stenning (1981: 224) refer to this as 'mutual consumption of ... services' (Davis, et al., 1991).

What Is the Focus in References?

In addition to *which* references are chosen, ideology plays a part in *how* they are presented. In composing sentences about previous research, there are two possible elements: the research **narrative** and the findings or claim, which I call the **phenomenon**, as in the following examples.

Narrative	Phenomenon
Smith (1977) found	Smoking causes cancer.
According to Jones (1980)	

1. The research narrative can be **expressed**:

   a. **and the researcher prominent** (as the subject of the sentence)

      - *Smith (1977) found* that smoking causes cancer.

Variant: in some journals, the author's first name (at first mention) and the name of the source are also included, as in:

- *Leo Bogart opens* The Age of Television *with an account of what he believes to be an event* ... (Sterne, 1999).

b. **The researcher can be expressed but not prominent** (not the subject of the sentence):

- Smoking causes cancer, *according to Jones (1980)*.

c. **the researcher (as agent) can be deleted**

- Smoking *has been found* to cause cancer (Smith, 1990).

- Smoking *has been found* to cause cancer[1].

Strictly speaking, *Smith* is deleted in both sentences above since the material in parentheses (*Smith, 1990*) is <u>not</u> part of the sentence. Nevertheless, neither style excludes the possibility of expressing the name of the researcher in the sentence, as in: *Smith (1990) found* ...[1]

2. Alternatively, **the phenomenon only can be expressed** and the research narrative omitted as in:

- Smoking causes cancer (Smith, 1990).

- Smoking causes cancer[1].

The result is that in (1), above, the research narrative is highlighted, while in (2) the phenomenon is highlighted. In order to judge rhetorical power, consider which form would have a greater chance of convincing the reader to stop smoking:

- Smith (1990) found that smoking causes cancer.

- Smoking causes cancer[1].

The phenomenon-prominent type of citation is in accord with Gilbert's description of empiricist discourse, in which "the facts speak for themselves" and the researcher is only a messenger (Gilbert, 1976). In contrast, in the Type 1 citation, in which the research narrative is highlighted, we acknowledge that facts are discovered and interpreted through human intervention and moreover, the identity of the researcher may be relevant. In particular, classical references are usually researcher-prominent, as in:

- Durkheim ([1897]/1951) considers the life-preserving functions of religion to be ... (Idler & Kasl, 1992: 1052).

Hyland's (1999) findings give good reason to believe that whether the researcher is expressed (*Smith found*) or suppressed (*Smoking causes cancer[1]*) varies with field. For instance, the researcher was expressed twice as frequently in citations in sociology than in physics. However, in general, in the majority of references in sociology, the researcher was <u>not</u> expressed (Hyland, 1999). In addition to these findings, it seems that in reviews, or parts of the review in which the purpose is to evaluate competing interpretations of phenomena or competing schools of thought, the researcher, not surprisingly, <u>is</u> prominent, as in:

> This claim is most strongly articulated by Marxist interpretations of Black Consciousness, although it is also present in liberal and pluralist readings. Baruch Hirson's analysis of the 1976 Soweto uprisings, for instance, dismisses the significance of Black Consciousness, arguing that .... A more nuanced and complex assessment of Black Consciousness is evident in Anthony Marx's recent book, *The Lessons of Struggle*, in which he acknowledges .... Furthermore, even in those accounts that do stress the more positive political effects of the BCM, such as those put forward by John Kane Berman, Gail Gerhart and Robert Fatton, there is little effort to specify the precise impact of the new ideology on the developing apartheid project during this period (Howarth, 1997).

Note that in the segment above, the author has kept the researchers prominent even though he has avoided making their names the grammatical subject of the sentence (Baruch Hirson's *analysis*, Anthony Marx's *recent book*). This adds variety to the writing and seems to deflect the criticism from the researchers themselves to their texts (*analysis, recent book, accounts*).

Along with field, the form of a reference sometimes reflects its location in the authors' argument; as they reach their hypothesis authors move from references in which the phenomenon is prominent to references in which the researcher is prominent. This observation has been validated for biomedical texts by Dubois (1980).

What Verbs Are Used?

If the author chooses to express the research-narrative structure, a reporting verb is necessary, as in *Smith states that* .... Here, Hyland's (1999) research again shows a variation among disciplines, with the most frequent verbs in sociology articles being *argue, suggest, describe, note, analyze,* and *discuss.* In contrast, in physics, the preferred verbs are *develop, report,* and *study.* The verbs *argue* and *discuss* reflect a greater emphasis on competing interpretations rather than on raw findings. In fact, in Hyland's (1999) corpus, the verb *argue* was found <u>only</u> in social science and the humanities. It would follow that each field has its own preferred verbs and there may be a difference even between sociology and other social sciences.

Patterns of Organization

As with everything else, there are many variations in how references can be organized. Some reviews are presented in groups of opposing theories. For example:

> **Two theories,** proposed to account for feeling-of-knowing judgments, are investigated here (see [citations] for reviews). **The target retrievability hypothesis** is based on the intuitive feeling that an item may be on the 'the tip of the tongue'. The hypothesis states that …. (see [citations] for such explanations). **Alternatively, the familiarity hypothesis** states that … Cue familiarity has been offered as an explanation of feeling-of-knowing by [citations] … [emphasis added]
>
> Several experiments have presented evidence that favor the cue familiarity hypothesis. [followed by references to specific experiments]
> ….
>
> Other experiments have produced data that are more consistent with the target retrievability hypothesis [citations].

This now leads very nicely into the authors' own contribution:

> The present experiments contrast the two hypothetical accounts of feeling of knowing (Schwartz & Metcalfe, 1992).

Before Writing the Review of Literature

Before you write, carefully study texts in your target genre and answer the following:

1. What proportion of the text is devoted to the review? Where is it located in the text (e.g., in a separate section or scattered throughout the introduction)?

2. How is the review organized, e.g., from stating the general phenomenon to mentioning specific variables involved in the study, or in terms of alternative schools of thought as in Schwartz & Metcalfe (1992) above?

3. To recall, I've mentioned 2 primary options in referring to previous research:

   a. *Smith (1990) found that smoking causes cancer.*

   b. *Smoking causes cancer (Smith, 1990) or Smoking causes cancer[1]*

   In the reviews of literature in your journals/field, in which cases is the researcher expressed, as in (a)? In which cases is only the phenomenon expressed, as in (b)?

4. Do the authors compliment certain research, as in: The *classical* paper of D & J; J & C *successfully* applied ...; B (1999) made *important* progress by ....?

Is there any pattern to these compliments?

5. Notice the typical reporting verbs used to introduce a theory and findings. Don't try to be original and **don't** use the thesaurus. If you are not a native speaker of English, you may be led astray. For instance, although they all can introduce claims, some verbs may be viewed as an invitation to combat, such as *admit, allege, contend, concede*. (It is better to be boring than rude!)

Guidelines for Writing the Review

After you have chosen the relevant, rhetorically, ideologically and politically correct references, your next job is to integrate them in a logical and interesting manner.

1. Decide what the contribution of each reference is. Remember, even if you have included some locally and internationally prominent names just to be polite, you should show how they fit into the overall debate, rather than just list them as if they were actors in a theatre program. In addition, clarify the connection between references, as in:

   Forsyth's (1979) study of the relationship between [x] and [y] found nurses had moderate to high empathy and that scores were higher for baccalaureate nurses when compared with diploma level nurses. (5) **Similarly,** Iwasiw and Olston (1985), ... found it was baccalaureate prepared nurses who were more empathic ... (6) **The results from both these studies suggest** that ...

2. When there are several references on one topic, organize them into groups and make a general statement about what will follow, as in:

   Investigation of the effectiveness of interpersonal communication skills training for nurses ... has provided some encouraging results. In the study by Anderson and Gerrard (1984), first year students ... were assessed relative to a control group. ... More recently Daniels et al., (1988) demonstrated the efficacy of a microcounselling program for teaching therapeutic communication skills to nurses (Sellick, 1991) [emphasis added]. (See a more complete version at the end of this chapter.)

   Conversely, if you want to combine several references in one sentence, make clear exactly who is responsible for each part, as in:

   Means-ends analysis is a 'content-free' (Bhaskar & Simon, 1977) problem-solving strategy for limiting the number of possible paths

to the solution **(Chi & Glaser, 1985; Greeno, 1980; Mayer, 1983)** (Zook
& Di Vesta, 1989) [emphasis added].

Notice also that the references within parentheses are listed in alphabetical,
not chronological, order, as recommended by the APA manual.

For the exact requirements for forms of citations, consult the style manual
used by your target journal. The name of the required manual is found
under the Guide to Contributors in the journal. The manual tells you how
the sources should be cited in the text and in the list of References at the
end. The most commonly used manual for social science is that of the
American Psychological Association (APA). Parts of this manual can be
downloaded from the internet. Parts of the two other main style manuals,
that of the Modern Language Association and the Chicago Manual of
Style, can also be downloaded. For electronic texts, the Columbia Guide
to Online Style is useful.

3. For each reference, decide what you want to highlight – the research
   narrative or the phenomenon. If you wish to highlight the research
   narrative, avoid the monotony of *Smith found* …. *Jones reported* ….
   Cohen claims …. Vary your sentence structure, as in:

   - In their pilot study, J & S demonstrated that …,

   - As early as 1895, it was known that …

   The subject of the verb does not have to be the cited author. The subject
   can be the research product, as in *The findings suggest* … or: *Forsyth's
   (1970) study of the relationship between [x] and [y] found* … (Sellick,
   1991).

4. When the researcher is the subject of the sentence, vary the reporting
   verb. Furthermore, when choosing verbs, clarify whether you (the citing
   author) accept the previous author's conclusions. For instance:

   a. Jones <u>reported</u> that the earth is flat

   can be followed by 'However, this was later proven wrong' while

   b. Jones <u>showed</u> that the earth is flat

   cannot be refuted.

   In the following section, you will find categories of verbs, some categories
   drawn from diverse fields (Thompson & Ye, 1991) and my own research
   in sociology and psychology (Lewin, Fine, & Young, 2001). Again, choose
   the verbs used in your field to indicate the status of the information. You
   will want to add typical verbs as you run across them.

5. ☹ Remember: the rules about verb tenses still apply! (To review, see Chapter 3.)

- In 1997, Smith found

  but

- Recently, Smith (1997) has found …

Verbs that Report Claims and Information

(Verbs are given in base form)

1. If you, the citing author, **accept the information as true,** you can choose a verb such as the following:

   a. **with a human agent, as in:**

      - Jones *acknowledges* … that the earth is round.

        acknowledge, confirm, demonstrate, determine, discover, establish, find [always expressed as 'found'], identify, illuminate, indicate, notice, observe [in sense of 'find'], prove, recognize, reveal, show, solve, substantiate, validate, verify

   b. **with a non-human agent, as in:**

      - Jones' model/theory *accounts for* …

      - The findings *support* the theory that ….

2. If you **don't want to make a commitment as to whether the information is true,** you can choose a verb such as:

   a. **with human and non-human agents**

      - Jones & Brown/ the findings *suggest, explain*

   b. **with human agents only** (as of this writing, but who can tell what the future will bring?)

      - *argue, hypothesize, maintain, posit, postulate, propose, claim, conclude, reach a conclusion, think, suspect, speculate, presume*

3. If you **do not accept the position of a previous author:**

   - Jones *misunderstood* X.

   - Smith *overlooks/neglects* historical research.

     or

     When McLuhanite critics write of television's 'tactile' or 'instantaneous' qualities, they are *mistaking* the historical conditions of television for its fundamental nature (for example, see [citations]) (Sterne, 1999).

In general, I advise novice writers, who presumably are novice scientists, to steer clear of outright confrontations, whether through the verb or any other part of the sentence.

Verbs and Phrases of Comparison

Smith's findings *correspond to/are in accord with/are consistent with/contrast with/* those of Jones et al.

Verbs that Introduce Variables or the Purpose of the Study

Jones/ the research *advance, compare, consider, examine, investigate, test, study, utilize, provide, focus on*

Verbs that Introduce Research Methods

We *measure, calculate, quantify, obtain, analyze, extend* [someone's idea, findings], *explore, observe* [in the sense of *examine*], *compare, isolate, identify.* (**all these verbs require an object**)

Verbs that Preview General Text

a. **Non-human agents as in:**

 - Research *has documented* that ...,

b. **Human and non-human agents:**

 - Jones/ this article *report, note, present, describe*

Sample Review

The first draft of a review of literature submitted by students sometimes looks like this:

Nurses' interpersonal behaviours and the development of helping skills

Forsyth (1979) found nurses had moderate to high empathy and that scores were higher for baccalaureate nurses when compared with diploma level nurses.

Iwasiw and Olston (1985) found it was baccalaureate prepared nurses who were more empathic ....

Anderson and Gerrard (1984) found that first year students who participated in a comprehensive interpersonal skills course were more empathic than a control group that had received no training.

Daniels et al., (1988) demonstrated the efficacy of a microcounselling program for teaching therapeutic communication skills to nurses.

Below, you can see how an experienced author arranged these findings for the published version. Notice how groups of findings are preceded by organizing sentences and followed by summary statements. In addition, the connections between each two findings and between groups is clear. Thirdly, there is a variety of sentence patterns instead of the ubiquitous *Smith found...*, *Jones found....* Lastly, the phenomenon that is under study becomes increasingly more specific, almost as if a zoom lens has now been focused on part of the large picture of nurses' interpersonal skills. The author moves from the importance of interpersonal skills in general (sentence 1) to the relationship between interpersonal skills and specific characteristics of nurses, (4–6) and finally to interpersonal skills training in sentences (7–9), leading to the author's focus in this study. Furthermore, while the phenomenon is prominent at the most general level of focus, particular researchers are made prominent as the variables become more specific.

(I have omitted many sentences from this review in order to keep it brief and added sentence numbers for reference purposes.)

(1) It has long been acknowledged that interpersonal communication, helping, and counselling skills are a fundamental component of the nurses role and essential prerequisites for quality nursing care (3 citations). ... [*references support Move 1, Establishing Relevance*].

(2) The interpersonal qualities and communication skills of nurses have received scant research attention. (3) Further, findings from the few studies that have been published are disappointing ... (3 citations) [*author summarizes results*]

(4) However, not all studies present such a pessimistic view. [*shows connection to and summarizes next group of references*] (5) Forsyth's (1979) study of the relationship between [x] and [y] found nurses had moderate to high empathy and that scores were higher for baccalaureate nurses when compared with diploma level nurses. (5) Similarly, Iwasiw and Olston (1985), in their pilot study of acute care nurses, found it was baccalaureate prepared nurses who were more empathic .... (6) The results from both these studies suggest that helping attitudes can also vary as a function of age, years of experience, and field of nursing practice. [*again summarizes results and narrows down the author's proposed variables*]

(7) Investigation of the effectiveness of interpersonal communication skills training for nurses ... has provided some encouraging results. [*organizes information that will follow*] (8) In the study by Anderson and Gerrard (1984), first year students who participated in a comprehensive

interpersonal skills course were assessed relative to a control group ....
(9) More recently Daniels et al., (1988) demonstrated the efficacy of
a microcounselling program for teaching therapeutic communication
skills to nurses (Sellick, 1991: 3–4).

Tasks:

1. **Making Connections**

   The following excerpt, written by a student, has a good opening
   sentence but lacks connections. What is the connection between
   (3) and (4)? Also sentences 2, 3, and 4 follow the same pattern
   (N said that ....) Try to make this paragraph connected and less
   monotonous. See Chapter 6 on connectives.

   (1) Alcoholism is a family disease that influences all the family
   members (Emshoff and Anyan, 1991). (2) Steinglass (1996)
   claims that while one of the family members is an alcoholic
   all the family fits its daily life to his problem. (3) Black (1982)
   identifies within the alcoholic family 'three don'ts'—'Don't feel',
   'don't believe' and 'don't talk.'

   (4) Erikson (1950) describes 8 stages of human development
   which occur along the life cycle. One of them is forming the
   ego identity of the adolescent. Children of alcoholics can have
   difficulties in forming their 'ego identity' because of the effect of
   their parents (Ackerman, 1983).

2. **Integrating the Literature**

   Here is a list of references I read and their main findings. The
   subject is: 'Attitudinal Aspects of Immigrants' Choice of Home
   Language' or, in other words, do English speaking immigrants
   prefer to speak English to their children or the language of the
   host country? What factors go into their choice of language? The
   study attempted to assess the weight of all the components of
   attitude in the parents' decision. Some of the factors are:

   type of motivation
   ethnic identity
   properties of the language

   I have presented these references as a 'shopping list'. Write a
   review of the literature that integrates these findings. Remember
   to observe the rules given above: vary your sentence structure
   and show the connection between findings. Your stance can be
   that all these findings are 'true' or at least, accepted.

Arrange the references in any order you think justified. Add connecting sentences, conclusions, and whatever you think necessary.

type of motivation

___ Gardner & Lambert (1972): There are two basic kinds of motivation in learning an additional language. The *integrative* 'reflects an inquisitiveness and genuine interest in the people comprising a cultural group …. while the *instrumental* is characterized by a desire to gain social recognition or economic advantage through knowledge of a foreign language.'

___ Gardner & Lambert (1972): studied English-speaking students in Montreal; attitudes and intelligence were held constant; results = those students with an 'integrative' orientation were more successful in certain aspects of learning French than those with an 'instrumental' orientation.

___ Harrison (1980): studied bilingual (English-Welsh) mothers in Wales. Instrumental motives were predominant in mothers whose children grow up as monolinguals while integrative ones are stronger in mothers whose children eventually are bilingual

___ Lambert (1980): found that prejudice against the immigrant group is associated with weaker motivation to learn their language.

ethnic identity

___ Houlton & King (1985): studied immigrant parents in the U.K. Found that parental support for mother tongue instruction in the schools was balanced by fears of a negative influence on the child's English achievement.

___ Gilhotra (1985): studied immigrants in Australia. Found that parents preferred to have the children study their mother tongue. Reason—ethnic group maintenance

properties of the language

___ Cooper & Fishman (1974): people perceive that languages differ in their power as vehicles for religious or scientific messages.

___ Cooper & Fishman (1974): occasionally, a speech community negatively evaluates its own language.

___ Ferguson (1959): everyone thinks his own language is superior. However, every language group gives different reasons for the 'superiority' of their language.

___ Gibbons (1982): English represents access to the modern age, technology and international communication.

___Lewis (1975): found that Welsh-English bilinguals associated Welsh with traditional and nationalistic considerations. They rated Welsh low when weighing practical considerations or beliefs about the viability of the Welsh language.

___ Stevens (1983): English is a reminder of past domination by a foreign power.

Notes:

[1] Indeed, after studying the misprints in citations, two authors concluded that only about 20% of citers had actually read the original article they cited. They had copied the reference (including the misprints) from a secondary source (Simkin & Roychowdhury, 2003).

Chapter 9

Methods

Structure

The Methods section has various titles, such as "Data & Variables" and "Procedures". Regardless of the title, this section, like Introductions and Discussions, has a prototypical structure, below. Of course, there are many possible variations, depending upon the type of research, (e.g., experimental or *post facto*), journal style, and so on. Therefore, you will need to determine the structure of the Methods section in your target genre, such as journal article or research proposal. The section devoted to Methods usually includes descriptions of the sample and how it was chosen, of the measures used to collect the data, and of the data analysis.

Setting

When relevant, the authors describe the geographical area or social system (such as hospital or university) in which the study took place.

Sample

This element explains how the sample was chosen, e.g., *randomly assigned to groups*. If customary, you may need to clarify the question of whether the sample was representative, as in:

> The sample was a randomly selected group drawn from [name of population, e.g., students taking the course]. These 225 respondents comprise a fairly representative sample of this population.

Relevant demographic characteristics of the sample (such as ages and gender) are included and possibly summarized in the first one or two tables. For example:

- This sample consisted of a random selection of 1,000 live twin births in each year cohort between 1985 and 1988 (Liang & Eley, 2005: 1249).

Measures/Instruments/Materials/Apparatus

The following excerpt illustrates a succinct way of (1) naming the instrument; (2) describing its function; (3) claiming its appropriateness for the task; (4) giving its source.

> *Life event measure* (1) 'The Life Event Scale for Adolescents' (LES-A) (Coddington, 1984) was used to assess negative life events for the past year. (2) This is a simple count of the number of life events an adolescent has experienced over the past year from a list of 50 events, (3) and has been shown to be reasonably reliable and valid (4) (Coddington, 1984) (Liang & Eley, 2005: 1250).

If you used scales, explain what the points on the scale represent:

- Each item solicited responses along a five point Likert type format (1—strongly disagree; 5—strongly agree)

Describe Your Instrument

> Questionnaires
>
> A bilingual version of the questionnaire (English/Spanish) was administered. The 15 items of the questionnaire (see Appendix XX) deal with the following variables:
>
> 1.
>
> 2. (etc.)

Procedure/Design

From your model articles, determine how much detail is necessary. Is it sufficient to say *'Participants were chosen randomly'* or should you specify exactly how you selected the participants? Try to anticipate your readers' questions. Of course, the best time to anticipate possible questions is while you are planning your study. The APA manual (2001) advises you to give enough detail so that the procedure could be replicated. (See Chapter 5, Being Concise.)

Statistical Analysis

Similarly to Measures, the authors describe the statistical measures [1] and their rationale, [2], below. The procedure is then described in detail.

> [1] The data were analyzed with a series of univariate and multivariate linear regression analyses using the statistical analysis package STATA (Stata Corportion, 2002) .... The third phase of analyses involved repeating Phase 2 using MZ twin difference measures [2] to exclude the effects of genetic vulnerability and shared environment (Table 4: columns a–c) (Liang & Eley, 2005: 1250–1).

Language Characteristics

Rationale

When necessary, the authors provide a rationale for their choice of sample, measures, or certain steps in the procedure and statistical analysis. The rationale is often introduced by phrases such as:

- We did XX …

    in order to test for X

    in an effort to characterize X

    to + verb, e.g., to determine why …

For example: [italics added]

> *To provide overall better discrimination at the lower end of the scale necessary for selection of groups with high and low depressive symptoms …, we devised a 4-point scale adaptation of the original 3-point scale* (Liang & Eley, 2005: 1249).

When writing the rationale, avoid making the experiment the 'agent', as in **This experiment attempted to demonstrate X.*

Prepositions

For those for whom English is a foreign language, perhaps the most difficult part of writing the Methods is finding the correct prepositions. I wish I could say there is a pattern to all this, but I don't really believe it. For instance, we say:

> the lecture ON UFOS will be given ON Monday, (or ON June 3), AT 3:00 p.m., IN the auditorium OF the university.

Here are some prepositions useful in describing methods:

Substitution:

- we used X in place OF/instead OF/Y
- we can substitute nuclear energy FOR oil

Capability:

- this algorithm is capable OF

Composition:

- this method consists OF three steps
- my sample was composed OF two groups

Dependence:

- good health depends ON good food
- this theory is based ON

Rate:

- a rate OF 5 km per hour

Range:

- the ages ranged FROM 5 to15

Time:

- *at*: (a specific time) ten o'clock, noon
- *on*: (a day) Monday
- *in*: (within the time period) the evening, June, the summer, 1989, times of crisis

Locations:

- *A place*: I will meet you AT the café/the clock/the entrance (not necessarily IN the café)
- *A point*: water boils AT 100 degrees
- *A line*: ON the X axis
- *A surface*: ON the wall
- *Area*: IN the country, room

Agents, Instruments:

- This experiment was done BY someone
- This experiment was done BY x method

Describing the Sample:

The sample was composed OF two groups OF 22 undergraduates AT a large university. They were members OF a course IN interpersonal behavior taught BY the author IN the fall of 2004. The mean age OF the group was 21. The course met three times a week FOR one hour DURING one academic semester. The students filled IN a questionnaire that consisted OF three parts. They did not have to write their names ON the questionnaire.

Showing Sequence

If the chronological order of the steps is important, use expressions such as: *previously, hitherto* (i.e., until this moment), *next, then, afterwards, subsequently, later*.

Describing a Sample

The sample is described in terms of demographic measures (*the children*) or variables (*the people who had not undergone training*). Be sure to follow the custom in your field. For instance, are people who are injured in traffic accidents referred to as *automobile accident victims* or as *victims of a motor vehicle crash*? The wording may also influence how the article is later indexed in the data base. Once you have the suitable phrase, be consistent throughout your article.

What is your opinion of a sentence such as *The manic-depressive subjects were treated with XYZ*? This was once a perfectly good sentence, but almost every word (except XYZ) is now unacceptable. As mentioned in Chapter 1, Constraints, many writing 'rules' emanate not from grammar but from social conventions. Perhaps some of the most interesting changes have occurred in the way we describe people being studied. This is not just a matter of being 'politically correct' but showing a greater sensitivity to them as human beings, as well as representing them as equal to everyone else in society.

For instance, since the 1994 APA guidelines, people in an experiment are no longer to be referred to as *subjects* but as *participants* in the study with the asumption that they exercised free will about being included in the research. (People who are interviewed or fill out questionnaires are *respondents*.) Secondly, as mentioned in Chapter 2, unless you are dealing with only one sex, the participants should be referred to by both masculine and feminine pronouns, or by plural forms:

- The children were given a task. *They* had to ….

Thirdly, an orientation toward the same sex or towards the opposite sex must be treated equally, with no aspersions about the 'normality' of a particular orientation. Finally, people are no longer referred to by their disability, e.g., *the manic-depressives* or *the deaf*, as if they have no other characteristics. The preferred term is *patients with manic-depressive illness*. If you are dealing with one of these 'special' populations, consult the APA guidelines for the recommended language. If there are no guidelines for a particular group, follow the pattern in your target journal.

Describing What You Did

Special verbs—*to perform* an analysis; *to administer* tests, to *collect, code, analyze* data; *to calculate, compute* correlations and statistical tests

Passive or active—the APA manual stipulates that you do not use the passive voice when describing how you dealt with the participants in your study, as in *Participants were fed hamburgers*. This is not because it hides the agent, for it is understood that the author was the agent, but because the APA rightly feels the grammatical passive confers upon the participant the status of a passive (and perhaps coerced) actor in the experiment.

It is pretty hard to avoid the passive in the methods section, unless one writes '*We did this. We did that*', which would be very monotonous. We can find a happy medium, as in the following excerpt, which alternates between passive and active voice:

> Data were collected from Loss Prevention incident reports ... during 1986, 1987, and 1988. For each case, we recorded whether the person was arrested or placed on civil recovery. We also recorded the date of the apprehension ... (Davis, Lundman & Martinez, 1991).

Notice if your journal uses the passive or a combination of active and passive sentences.

Compression

Language in the Methods section tends to be very compressed. One way to compress language but not lose any information is to transform passive verbs into adjectives. The following sentences show how this is done.

- We interviewed 270 people. They constitute a sample that is representative of the population.

  1. Change the first sentence to passive

     - 270 people were interviewed....

  2. Combine the two sentences by a wh-clause, i.e., a clause beginning with a relative pronoun (*who, which*, or *that*), which gives us:

     - The 270 people who were interviewed constitute a sample that is representative of the population.

  3. The relative pronoun and verb *to be* can be deleted so that we get:

     - The 270 people interviewed constitute a sample representative of the population.

Interviewed now becomes an adjective describing the people; the main verb is now *constitute*. This also changes the balance of information so that *interviewed* is now secondary order information and *constitute a sample* is primary.

Here is another example of the process of compressing two sentences:

- We obtained data from the 2000 census. These data proved to be inaccurate.

  1. Change the first sentence to passive

     - Data from the 2000 census were obtained ....

2. Combine the two sentences by adding a wh-clause:

- Data from the 2000 census were obtained that proved to be inaccurate.

3. Delete the relative pronoun and the verb *to be* (*were*):

- Data obtained from the 2000 census proved to be inaccurate.

Ethical Considerations

Besides describing the participants in sensitive language, above, authors have to reassure readers that the participants were actually treated with respect and certain ethical and legal requirements were observed. Thus, the Methods section often includes statements such as:

> Anonymity and confidentiality were assured and stressed to all participants. (Informed) consent was obtained from participants (or their guardians).

In experiments in which the participants are exposed to any negative experiences, you should explain how you relieved participants of any anxiety that may have accrued from their research experience. In the following example, the authors tested eight to ten-year-old boys under 'relaxed' and 'threatening' conditions. The authors assure us, in the Methods section, that there were no after-effects:

> Finally, the subject* was fully debriefed about the procedure and told the purpose of the study. Specific caution was exercised to ensure that the subject understood the procedure and its goal and that no residual effect remained. The subject was praised for his participation and was asked to refrain from telling peers about the study. All subjects agreed to this request. The experimenter checked with the classroom teacher to make sure that subjects did not display behavior indicating that they were upset and did not inform peers about the procedure. The experimenter and the teachers were convinced that subjects were not adversely affected (Dodge & Somberg, 1987: 217).

*This article was written before the change in APA guidelines.

As a general guideline, keep in mind Bem's (1987: 182) admonition that readers should be assured that participants:

> left your study with their self-esteem intact and their respect for you and psychology enhanced rather than diminished.

Similarly, if you use animals, you must indicate that they were handled compassionately.

Task: Writing Methods

1. Determine the structure of the Methods section in your target genre/journal.

In about three paragraphs:

2. Give operational definitions of your variables, such as *Depression [or drug abuse] was defined as:*

3. describe your instruments

4. describe your procedure

Chapter 10

Results

This chapter discusses the Results section when it is not combined with the Discussion section in the research report. In my study of the literature, two surprising findings emerged. If size is any indication, the Results section is sometimes the most important section. In a study of 20 articles chosen at random from five sociology journals, Brett (1994) determined that the largest section (40% of the article) was Results, followed by the Introduction, Method, and Discussion.

Secondly, although we are taught that Results should contain only objective descriptions of the data, with no interpretation or comments by the author,[1] I have found comments in Results, such as *unfortunately, unexpectedly, surprisingly, remarkably* and even '*The most shocking findings of the study* ….'

Brett (1994) also found that sociology articles are not restricted to 'pure' presentation of the data but contain other moves, which we expect to be an integral part of the Discussion, as discussed in Chapter 11. In addition to stating results and restating the hypotheses, authors also offer their own interpretation, comment and opinion about the results already presented. Specifically, Brett found the following Discussion type moves:

- comparing findings to previous studies

- raising further questions about, and/or discuss implications of the results

- claiming agreement with previous studies

- commenting on the data

- admitting difficulties in interpretation

- pointing out unexpected results

- calling for further research

Results also included 'justifying the procedure', (e.g., *To test for X, we analyzed Y*), a move associated with Methods. Similarly, these findings have been confirmed by analyses done by my own students. Lest we think sociology is 'deviant', a similar finding is true of biochemistry texts (Thompson, D., 1993).

119

If this is true of other social sciences, it may mean that authors find that reporting only 'pure' results is contrary to the way an argument should be presented. It seems more reasonable to remind the audience what each result may mean rather than postpone the implications until the Discussion section, where, again the Results have to be summarized. Swales and Feak (1994: 171) argue that this practice may reflect authors' awareness of their unseen audience, anticipating

> that their readers may be thinking 'Why did they use this method rather than that one?' or 'Isn't this result rather strange?' … authors may not want to postpone responding to such imaginary questions and critical comments until the final section.

Based on this reasoning, one wonders why all journals do not require Results and Discussion to be combined in one section. You need to determine the prevailing system in your discipline and follow it, even it means adding some discussion to your Results section.

Presenting Data in Graphics or Images (Visuals)

Some fields need to present statistical data. This move consists of two parts: presenting the actual data in a table or figure and then directing readers' attention to it. There are different ways to point to data. Interestingly, each type of sentence structure seems to have a different rhetorical impact, analogous to the way information can be presented in the Review of Literature, Chapter 8.

'Container' of data is prominent:

1. *This model/table* shows/provides/gives/presents/illustrates/reveals/displays/depicts/indicates that ….

Data are prominent:

2. *The association between smoking and high mortality* is shown/indicated/presented/ in Table 1.

3. Smoking is associated with high death rates. (See Table 1.)

It seems well-advised to follow the guidance of the APA manual and generalize rather than repeat statistics from the tables. In the following example, the authors present their statistics as

- Table 4: Correlations between Emotional Intelligence and Social Environment Scores ….

They then summarize (rather than repeat) the results in the table:

> Relationships between EI and linguistic characteristics of writing about September 11th were evaluated using Pearson Product Moment correlations (see Table 4).

> Consistent with the hypothesis, use of affect words was positively correlated with the TMMS total score and scores on the Clarity of Emotion and Mood Repair subscales (Graves, Schmidt, & Andrykowski, 2005: 293).

A Word about Visuals

Much has been written about presenting visuals. In general, the appearance of visuals is not in the purview of this book, but for some relevant points, see Chapter 12, Conference texts, visuals. One point worth remembering is to choose the graphic form that will best highlight the statistical trends. For instance, look at Table 10-1, as it was originally published.

Table 10-1   Percentage of Songs Containing Stereotyped Images (in %)

Image	1946	1956	1966	1976
Woman as evil	9.6	17.2	28.6	24.2
Physical characteristics	6.4	11.7	13.6	20.4
Need for man	37.4	40.6	19.7	21.6
Possession of man	12.2	17.5	17.4	16.7
Woman as mother	7.8	8.8	2.3	14.9
Woman as sex object	22.9	21.8	15.0	23.8
Woman as delicate	14.8	9.4	13.6	13.0
Woman as childlike	26.4	26.0	48.8	45.5
Woman on a pedestal	3.8	4.5	5.6	4.5
Woman as attractive	4.1	4.5	8.0	4.8
Woman as supernatural	5.8	3.9	8.5	11.5

Source: Cooper (1985).

As a class exercise, one my students rearranged the data into categories and then plotted the categories over time in the graph in 10-1:

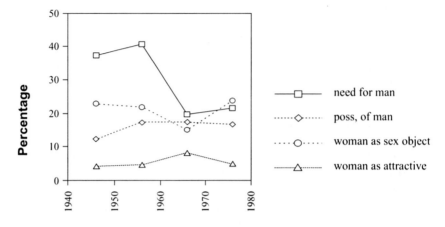

Figure 10-1   Women in Popular Music

This figure makes the point much more vividly than the table. We now clearly see the changes in styles of referring to women in popular songs.

Commenting on Visuals

Similarly, the verbal commentary on your visuals deserves careful thought. For example, consider Table 10-2, which displays the results of my imaginary survey. I asked 100 passersby, 'Who would you vote for in the next election?'

Table 10-2   Preferences for Candidates in Forthcoming Election

Name of Candidate	Party	% respondents
Jones	Yellow	05
Thompson	Yellow	39
Smith	Purple	18
Crook	Purple	33
Don't know		05

Of course, you would phrase the comment to conform to your hypothesis but for the sake of this point, notice that there are many ways to interpret these statistics.

- The most popular candidate is Thompson.

- The majority of voters would not vote for Thompson.

- The majority of voters prefer the Purple party.

Prepositions To Express Results

- X is related TO Y
  X is positively correlated WITH Y
  X is compared TO Y
  X has an effect ON Y
  X results IN Y
  X is a factor IN Y

- To account FOR this difference, we tested ….
  Cancer has been attributed TO smoking
  Cancer is a consequence OF smoking

Tasks: Writing Results

Study your model articles.

1. Which is the largest section? (Introduction, Methods, Results, or Discussion)

2. Are Results combined with Discussion or presented separately?

3. What is the order in which results are presented?

   - most significant to least significant

   - expected to unexpected

   - in order of the hypotheses

   - other: specify

4. Are there moves other than 'pure' reporting of results and showing tables? If so, what are they? (See Brett's list above.)

5. Is any special language used that we haven't mentioned so far?

6. How are statistics dealt with? Do the authors refer readers to the relevant visual, such as *Table 1 presents means and standard deviations for all variables* (Crowson, Thoma & Hestevold, 2005) or do they describe the statistics in detail?

7. Write a commentary to describe the statistics in Figure 10-1, 'Women in popular music'. Comment on each of the four trends.

Notes:

[1] The APA manual (2001: 20) advises 'Report the data in sufficient detail to justify the conclusions .... Discussing implications is NOT appropriate here'.

Chapter 11

Discussion Sections

This chapter attempts to answer two questions:

1. What are the usual moves in a Discussion section and their rhetorical functions?

2. What lexical and grammatical structures are common to these moves?

The essential parts of a research text are the report of the author's findings and enough of a description of his methods that the research could be replicated. Indeed, these are the core of the earliest texts in English, as the following report communicated to the Royal Society in 1717 attests.

> According to these laudable Examples [of Hippocrates, Galen and other Fathers of Medicine] I shall, for the Satisfaction of the Curious and Ingenious, give a true and faithful Account of an extraordinary Excrescence cut off from the cheek of a Man ....

In his conclusion, in contrast with today's authors, the writer carefully refrains from making any interpretation.

> I have given a true and plan Account of this extraordinary Case from certain Information; I have contented myself to relate only Matters of Fact, without making any Observations or Reflections on it for I leave it to the Philosophers and Virtuosi to make their own Reasonings and Refinements as seems best to themselves (Valle, 1997: 86).

However, today, such a report of bare facts does not suffice; it must be prefaced by an Introduction, carefully motivating the research, and concluded with a Discussion section, validating, justifying, and sometimes extolling the findings. In fact, according to Hyland (1999: 343):

> Historical research on scientific texts has demonstrated the gradual emergence of the Discussion section to replace Methods as the dominant basis of persuasion.

There are variations according to journal. Sometimes Discussions are combined with Results (which seems to be a much more logical system); sometimes Discussion is labeled 'Conclusions'. Regardless of how it's labeled, a research report would be incomplete without a Discussion. Furthermore, we recognize Discussions by the existence of certain predictable elements (moves).

First, please reread Chapter 7, Understanding Genre Analysis. As is the Introduction, the Discussion is presented in a predictable format. (You can see that the text quoted above by Valle does not satisfy our expectations for a Discussion.) Let's look at a contemporary text, from which I've deleted many details, and try to mark out about five major moves (as we did on Introductions, in Chapter 7). What do you think is the purpose of each of the moves you've found? What words gave you the signal for that move? After you've done this, the section below, *What are the moves and their rhetorical functions?* will make more sense to you.

EXAMPLE TEXT

Complicated grief and bereavement-related depression as distinct disorders: Preliminary empirical validation in elderly bereaved spouses

DISCUSSION [authors' label]

In these analyses we attempted to identify a cluster of symptoms that might be interpreted as indicators of complicated grief. The results suggest that complicated grief is distinct from bereavement-related depression. By demonstrating that this cluster of symptoms is significantly associated with longer-term functional impairment, we have attempted to show that the concept of complicated grief has both predictive validity and practical utility.

In considering these results, however, a few limitations must be kept in mind. First, the exclusion criteria and recruitment strategies may have had an influence on the type of subjects obtained for the study. Although our study group had representative scores on measures of grief and depression, the exclusion of patients with severe medical illness or prior psychopathology may have removed the subjects most vulnerable to complicated grief reactions, functional impairments, or bereavement-induced psychosis. In this way, study group selection biases may have resulted in the underestimation of complicated grief reactions and may have reduced our power to detect significant effects of complicated grief on follow-up measures of functioning.

Furthermore, while recruitment *efforts* were uniform for all subjects, and the distinction between depressed and nondepressed subjects was made post hoc, the *results* of the recruitment process revealed systematic differences in the means of entry into the study that varied according to the subjects' depression status. Sixty percent of the subjects who were depressed when they entered the study were solicited through the media and by word of mouth (e.g., through neighbors, friends, or staff members of Western Psychiatric Institute and Clinic), and 40% were clinically referred. All of the subjects who were not depressed at entry were obtained through media announcements and by word of mouth. Because the subjects who were not depressed at study entry were solicited rather than clinically referred, one might suspect that they had better health or higher levels of social functioning than the clinically referred subjects. When we examined the correlates of mode of recruitment, however, we found that the subjects who were clinically referred did not differ significantly from those responding to media or word-of-mouth solicitations with respect to levels of medical illness burden or social support.

Second, [limitation] ....

Third, because some subjects entered the study less than 6 months after the death of their spouses, these results do not provide an optimal test of the hypothesis that those who have high scores on complicated grief 6 months after their spouse's death will be most at risk for impaired long-term functioning. We would have preferred to use the scores obtained 6 months after the loss of a spouse because clinical experience and research (41) have shown that symptoms of grief decline significantly and reach low levels between the 4th and 6th months after loss. ... Nevertheless, the subjects available to us came from a study initially designed to examine EEG sleep in bereavement and bereavement-related depression, in which depressed subjects were subsequently treated with nortriptyline (31). Allowing a broader range of months since loss at baseline enabled us to approximately double the number of available subjects. In addition, intake assessments were obtained before treatment began. The inclusion of these subjects (many of whom would improve in their grief-related symptoms by the 6-month assessment) therefore should have provided a conservative test of our hypothesis.

A final point should be made concerning the assessments of these symptoms. Most bereavement researchers argue that it is not the type, but rather the severity, of grief symptoms that makes a grief reaction pathological (2, 11, 42). Our formulation of criteria for complicated grief differs from past work in that we think that specific symptoms will help to distinguish complicated from uncomplicated grief reactions. This is a marked departure from the opinion of the creators of the Texas Revised Inventory of Grief (12), who claim that "complicated grief reactions are often immediately obvious" (p. 111) because they are reflected in relatively higher total scores on their inventory. We do incorporate the notion of severity into our criteria because higher scores on our specific symptoms are expected to predict more extensive functional impairment, but we attempt to identify particular symptoms of complicated grief and not symptoms of grief in general.

... [details of explanation and comparison to previous literature]

The major finding of this study was that complicated grief, contrary to what many clinicians might have expected, emerged as a discrete set of symptoms that were relatively independent of the symptoms of bereavement-related depression. The results of the principal-components analysis revealed that ….

The results of this study also were consistent with Freud's assertion that diminished self-esteem is more a part of bereavement-related depression (melancholia) than of grief (mourning) (18). However, while Freud claimed that mourning was not pathological because it was not associated with a disturbance in "self-regard" (self-esteem), we have shown that mourning (complicated grief) can be pathological in that it predicts enduring functional impairment, despite the fact that impaired self-esteem is not a symptom of complicated grief.

Not only did the complicated grief factor appear to have content validity, but the results also indicated that it was reliable. Given that the symptoms were measured with a variety of instruments, the reliability of the complicated grief factor could not be attributed to the use of a single, internally consistent scale. Because the complicated grief factor assessed at baseline predicted global functioning, depressed mood, self-esteem, and self-reported sleep quality 18 months after the spouse's death, it appeared to have criterion validity as well. Evidently, the symptoms of complicated grief, while appearing to be normal reactions to the loss of a loved one, nevertheless were significantly associated with pathological outcomes. In light of its predictive validity, the diagnosis of complicated grief may have practical implications. If complicated grief predicts future dysfunction, then it should be identified, and specific treatment interventions should be developed for this condition.

CONCLUSIONS [authors' label]

In future research, investigation of the symptoms and consequences of complicated grief in a less select study group, where assessment is not potentially confounded by the effects of treatment, is needed. More robust results might be obtained with an assessment of complicated grief symptoms made 6 months after the death of the spouse rather than sooner. Once the construct of complicated grief is validated through replication in larger, more representative study groups, descriptive follow-up studies assessing life events, coping behaviors, social supports, gender differences, and other potentially relevant parameters could be used to identify factors associated with improvement in complicated grief. Ultimately, the treatment strategies based on this information will aim to decrease the symptoms associated with this disorder (separate from depression) and, thereby, increase the quality of life of the bereaved through enhanced physical, psychological, and social functioning (Prigerson et al., 1995: 27) [italics in the original].

What Are the Moves and Their Rhetorical Functions?

First, I will outline the 'ideal' structure of a Discussion section, and then we will compare it to the actual realization in the above text. The 'ideal' Discussion answers five main questions. The usual order, below, seems to be the most logical, working up from the past (what you found) to the future (what you recommend should be done). The answer to each of these questions constitutes a *move*. My labels for the moves appear in brackets, in capital letters (Lewin, Fine & Young, 2001).

1. What were your (the author's) main findings or main accomplishment? [REPORT MAJOR ACHIEVEMENTS] It's helpful to remind the reader of your results by providing a summary of results phrased in general (rather than quantitative or specific terms) even though they have been previously reported under the Results section.

   - 'The major finding of this study was that complicated grief ... emerged as a discrete set of symptoms ....' (Grief)

2. How well do your findings or methods fit hypotheses, methods, results of other studies, existing standards, accepted methods or measures for validity and reliability, and/or other criteria for research? [COMPARE FINDINGS TO ACCEPTED CRITERIA] For instance:

   - In sum, the unexpected effects of expressions were in every case consistent with other research on the dimensional structure and similarity among emotions (Duclos et al. 1989).

3. How do you interpret your findings? After presenting your research, you have to explain what it all means. According to Kerlinger (1973: 9):

   - [A] theory explains phenomena ... by specifying what variables are related to what variables and how they are related.

   [OFFER INTERPRETATION] It is said that in social science the interpretation is more important than the findings themselves. For instance:

   - It appears that the sex-role education of boys and girls is differentiated on the basis of affective response, rather than cognitive information (Fagot & Leinbach, 1989).

4. What problems or limitations may potential critics raise? Are there interpretations for the results alternative to the ones you have given? [WARD OFF POTENTIAL COUNTERCLAIMS] In the spirit of 'admit your defects before other people spot them', it is prudent to anticipate the issues first. Obviously, in a perfect world, you would discover the limitations while you are designing the study, but this is not a perfect

world. This move is analogous to 'establishing the gap' in Introductions. Here you are disclosing the possible gaps in your research; these gaps can be 'plugged' by recommending future research. Presumably, in the past, when the author reported research in the presence of potential critics, the response was immediate and actual as this extract attests:

> In a communication ... that was read before the Royal Society, January 8, 1863, I brought forward experimental evidence which had conducted me to view the immunity .... The opposition that this view received on the evening of its announcement induced me to extend my experiments, and ... I have deemed it desirable to present this further communication, in which the whole subject is concisely reviewed with the aid of the new matter that has been brought to light (Valle, 1997: 92).

In today's texts, the move 'ward off counterclaims' may be a vestige of such events as described above, transformed into an imaginary dialogue between you and projected critics. In this move, you anticipate potential criticism by the audience, state it clearly and then respond, either by dismissing it or accepting responsibility. In the 'Grief' text, the authors accept responsibility for at least one limitation:

> Third, because some subjects entered the study less than 6 months after the death of their spouses, these results do not provide an optimal test of the hypothesis that those who have high scores on complicated grief 6 months after their spouse's death will be most at risk for impaired long-term functioning. We would have preferred to use the scores obtained 6 months after the loss of a spouse.

Authors sometimes admit a limitation, but avoid accepting responsibility, by attributing the limitation to problems in the field, rather than in their own individual research, as in:

a. In their present form, routine activities ... theories are basically unfalsifiable since ... (Miethe, Stafford, & Long, 1987);

or

b. These contradictory results may be due to the limited generalizability of sleep laboratory studies or to ... (Hughes & Hatsukami, 1986).

5. What are the implications of your study? [STATE IMPLICATIONS] At least one previous author is recorded as protesting such a move:

- Because [the study of motivation] is a high and hazardous undertaking, I wish fewer people would meddle with it (Montaigne, 1580: 126, cited in Bem, 1987).

In spite of this injunction, modern authors often end their Discussion with implications, especially for research.

Implications include recommendations for future research, for a change in the theoretical stance of the discipline, and/or for changes in social policy to reflect the results of the study. You might notice a parallel here to Move 1 of Introductions, where relevance is established for the theoretical questions in research or for practical problems in human behavior; (see Chapter 7, Move 1). Making no recommendations for further research suggests that the work is complete. You might want to recommend further research even when you have discerned no possible flaws in the research. It indicates that the present research can be expanded or even improved upon, laying the groundwork for future studies.

Variability of Moves

Not all the moves appear in every text; for example, 'offer interpretation' may not be realized because an extensive explanation for the hypothesis has been offered in the Introduction, or because the expected relation was not found among the variables. Similarly, whether or not to compare the findings to previous literature may depend upon the existence of similar research that has to be acknowledged. However, either an interpretation OR a warding off of counterclaims appears in every Discussion text I've studied. (As I mentioned in Chapter 7 on Introductions, all the typical structures of a particular genre are not realized in every text, though some structures are obligatory.) So while the typical elements are the products of social convention, in writing as in preparing dinner, one is allowed a great deal of latitude. Similarly, returning to the 'dinner' analogy, we expect a 'usual' order from either an author or a host, but they can change the order, within certain limits. They cannot start a text with 'implications' or a dinner with dessert; if these items appear, they must be last. The other point worth mentioning is that the space devoted to each move is not uniform within one Discussion or across all Discussion texts. In the 'grief' text below, the authors seem to anticipate a lot of criticism of their study, while in other texts, the emphasis is on implications for future research. In the text on grief, there are variations in order and emphasis, but the moves I've outlined appear. How do they compare with your analysis?

I've tried to focus on major moves (in uppercase letters) with submoves in lowercase letters. I've also indicated the signals for each move in bold face, and the accompanying hedges, (toning down) by underlining.

Analysis of Example Text

Complicated Grief and Bereavement-Related Depression as Distinct Disorders: Preliminary Empirical Validation in Elderly Bereaved Spouses

Restate purpose of the study:

> In these analyses **we attempted to identify** a cluster of symptoms that <u>might be</u> interpreted as indicators of complicated grief. [*This conforms to the authors' introductory aim*: we were interested in developing criteria for the assessment of complicated grief]

OFFER INTERPRETATION

> **The results suggest** that complicated grief is distinct from bereavement-related depression. [*compare to hypothesis in Introduction*: we expect that complicated grief will emerge as a clinical entity distinct from bereavement-related depression.] ….

REPORT MAJOR ACHIEVEMENTS

This move can include results as in [a] and 'achievements' that are not technically results, as in [b].

[a] By demonstrating that this cluster of symptoms is significantly associated with longer-term functional impairment, we have attempted to show that

[b] the concept of complicated grief has both predictive validity and practical utility.

Notice the difference in level of generalization between the findings as reported above in [a] and in an excerpt from the Results section, below:

> The complicated grief factor was significantly associated with several aspects of functioning 18 months after the spouse had died, controlling for the number of months since the death at study intake. The complicated grief factor significantly predicted global functioning, depressed mood, self-reported sleep quality, and self-esteem 18 months after the loss of the spouse.

WARD OFF POTENTIAL COUNTERCLAIMS

> In considering these results, **however, a few limitations** must be kept in mind.

Raise potential counterclaim:

> First, the exclusion criteria and recruitment strategies <u>may have had</u> an influence on the type of subjects obtained for the study.

Respond to counterclaim:

The authors seem to accept the counterclaim, by offering no response (justification):

> Although our study group had representative scores on measures of grief and depression, the exclusion of patients with severe medical illness or prior psychopathology <u>may have removed</u> the subjects most

vulnerable to complicated grief reactions, functional impairments, or bereavement-induced psychosis. In this way, study group selection biases <u>may have resulted</u> in the underestimation of complicated grief reactions and <u>may have reduced</u> our power to detect significant effects of complicated grief on follow-up measures of functioning.

Raise another potential counterclaim:

... Because the subjects who were not depressed at study entry were solicited rather than clinically referred, **<u>one might suspect that</u>** they had better health or higher levels of social functioning than the clinically referred subjects.

Dismiss this counterclaim:

When we examined the correlates of mode of recruitment, however, we found that **the subjects who were clinically referred did not differ significantly** from those responding to media or word-of-mouth solicitations with respect to levels of medical illness burden or social support.

Raise potential counterclaim (2):

Second, ...

Raise potential counterclaim (3):

Third, ...

Raise potential counterclaim (4):

A final point should be made concerning the assessments of these symptoms. Most bereavement researchers argue that it is not the type, but rather the severity, of grief symptoms that makes a grief reaction pathological (2, 11, 42).

Dismiss counterclaim:

Our formulation of criteria for complicated grief differs from past work in that <u>we think</u> that specific symptoms will help to distinguish complicated from uncomplicated grief reactions. This is a marked departure from the opinion of the creators of the Texas Revised Inventory of Grief (12), who claim that "complicated grief reactions are often immediately obvious" (p. 111) because they are reflected in relatively higher total scores on their inventory. We do incorporate the notion of severity into our criteria because higher scores on our specific symptoms are expected to predict more extensive functional impairment, but we attempt to identify particular symptoms of complicated grief and not symptoms of grief in general. ... [details of explanation and comparison to previous literature]

REPORT MAJOR ACHIEVEMENTS [Reiterate]:

The major finding of this study was that complicated grief, contrary to what many clinicians might have expected, emerged as a discrete set of symptoms that were relatively independent of the symptoms of bereavement-related depression. The results of the principal-components analysis revealed that ....

COMPARE FINDINGS TO ACCEPTED CRITERIA:

(to literature):

The results of this study also were consistent with Freud's assertion that diminished self-esteem is more a part of bereavement-related depression (melancholia) than of grief (mourning) (18). However, **while Freud claimed that** mourning was not pathological because it was not associated with a disturbance in "self-regard" (self-esteem), **we have shown that** mourning (complicated grief) can be pathological in that it predicts enduring functional impairment, despite the fact that impaired self-esteem is not a symptom of complicated grief.

(to standards):

Not only did the complicated grief factor <u>appear</u> **to have content validity, but the results also indicated that it was reliable.** Given that the symptoms were measured with a variety of instruments, the reliability of the complicated grief factor could not be attributed to the use of a single, internally consistent scale. Because the complicated grief factor assessed at baseline predicted global functioning, depressed mood, self-esteem, and self-reported sleep quality 18 months after the spouse's death, it <u>appeared</u> to have criterion validity as well. <u>Evidently,</u> the symptoms of complicated grief, while <u>appearing</u> to be normal reactions to the loss of a loved one, nevertheless were significantly associated with pathological outcomes.

STATE IMPLICATIONS:

In light of its predictive validity, the diagnosis of complicated grief <u>may have</u> practical implications. If complicated grief predicts future dysfunction, then it should be identified, and specific treatment interventions should be developed for this condition.

CONCLUSIONS [in this section, the authors actually STATE IMPLICATIONS]:

[Notice that recommending what needs to be done implies acceptance of some of the potential counterclaims]

[for research]:

In future research, investigation of the symptoms and consequences of complicated grief in a less select study group, where assessment

is not potentially confounded by the effects of treatment, is needed. More robust results <u>might be obtained</u> with an assessment of complicated grief symptoms made 6 months after the death of the spouse rather than sooner. …

[for human behavior]:

Ultimately, the treatment strategies based on this information will aim to decrease the symptoms associated with this disorder (separate from depression) and, thereby, increase the quality of life of the bereaved through enhanced physical, psychological, and social functioning.

The Rhetorical Dimension of the Key Moves

The formal structure I've presented represents the bare bones of a Discussion. Don't forget that your purpose is to persuade your audience that significant work has been done. At the same time, you must attend to interpersonal relations involved by not appearing immodest or critical of others, especially if you are questioning the currently accepted theory. I spend much time talking about hedging (below) but let's not overdo it! Sometimes I have to remind students that the point is to report their accomplishments NOT their failures. In the following example, instead of emphasizing her accomplishments, a student ended the report of her research thusly:

It might be argued that X in its present form does not give a complete, profound answer to the present changes and challenges in health care settings. Maybe additional meetings, in small groups, may help the assimilation of the topics into day to day reality.

Even if there are many limitations, make sure to stress the positive aspect of what you've done. In the following example, a student found statistical differences in patients' reactions to the first and second occurrence of a disease but he wasn't sure that these results would be of practical help. He wrote:

- We are not convinced that our results are also clinically significant.

This would make a reader of the target social work journal wonder why this research was published at all. After our discussion, the student rewrote the section clarifying that certain groups are more at risk for PTSD and other distress symptoms.

The five moves in the Discussion section represent a continuum from reporting 'facts' to addressing interpersonal needs. *Report achievements* centers on reality (what the authors found), while at the other end, *ward off counterclaims* and, to a lesser degree, *state implications*, are responses to subjective and interpersonal considerations. *Ward off counterclaims* can be said to have been created solely to deal with the relations between author (scientist) and audience (colleagues). *Compare findings to accepted criteria* allows for varying degrees of judgment about the 'fitness' of one's claims/conclusions.

One can say they fit other research: (with *consistent* being very common in this context)

- In sum, the unexpected effects of [x] were consistent with other research …

or they do not quite fit other research:

- Although these results are somewhat contradictory to those of W et al, …,

or they may be superior to other research, as in:

> We believe the validity of our results is greater than that of prior studies for several reasons …. We also believe the results of our study are more generalizable than those of prior retrospective surveys … to our knowledge, the present study is the first to document observable changes … (Hughes & Hatsukami, 1986).

or one was frankly surprised by the results:

> Although the results fit the general multidimensional expectations quite nicely, they were more complex than anticipated (Duclos et al., 1989).

As you can see, you must strike a judicious balance between your role as neutral observer and as emotionally involved participant, trying to persuade your audience of the success of the research.

Sequencing Arguments

Until now I've treated the Discussion section as consisting of one finding and all the adjacent moves elaborating on that one finding. If you have many findings, look for a model to see how these are treated. You might find that findings are discussed separately as in these created examples:

FINDING 1

[Summarize result]:

- Women tended to start abusing drugs at a later age than men

[Compare to accepted criteria]:

- This is consistent with previous research ….

[Interpret]:

- This may be due to the fact that women live in more protected environments … etc.

FINDING 2

[Summarize result]:

- Women tended to abuse alcohol more than men ....

[Compare to accepted criteria]:

- This is in contrast with previous research , which found that ....

[Interpret]

- The reason for this may be that women prefer the social atmosphere in which drinking is popular ... etc.

Alternatively, instead of separating your findings, you can combine them into a general summary, followed by a general statement comparing findings to other criteria, and so on, ending with implications of all the findings together, as the following example:

> In this study of privately hospitalized cocaine abusers, we found many similarities as well as several differences between the sexes. Our data revealed that the women we studied generally began using cocaine at a younger age ... (Griffin, Weiss, Mirin, & Lange, 1989).

followed by a list of findings and then the authors' interpretation and implications, which integrate all the findings.

After deciding on the formal structure of your results, you need to decide upon their order, i.e., which results should be prominent. Think about how you read a research text. Reread your hypothesis/es. Start the Discussion with a statement of whether your hypotheses were confirmed or not confirmed. Notice how the interpretation in the Discussion on grief, above, directly links with the hypothesis in the Introduction.

Although his book is directed to biologists, Lindsay (1994) offers several relevant tips for structuring a Discussion in any field, especially for structuring the summary of results. How can you show what is the most important result? His dictum to 'lead with your strongest argument' and result (p. 23) seems eminently sensible. In addition, as Lindsay reminds us, the reader expects a correlation between the proportion of text devoted to an argument or a result and its importance. It flows from that that minor points should not take up more space than major results. In addition, it is acceptable occasionally to signal the important findings, as in: 'The most important aspect of these results is ....'

As is true for everything you write, formulate your strong arguments in a clear topic sentence, ideally in the first sentence in the paragraph.

Lexical/Grammatical Structures

Hedging

One of my students, asked to describe his work, wrote the following:

> Our novel experimental technique enables us to determine [x] and [y] independently. The [y] values measured by us for ... are higher by nearly two orders of magnitude than the ones obtained for p type crystals. This fact was not taken into account by the authors of the above mentioned papers. In my opinion, this is the reason for their wrong conclusions.

The grammar, sentence structure, and register are excellent. But it strikes a jarring note for most English-speaking readers. Do you see a problem? If not, let me put it this way: would you want to invite this fellow to dinner? He may be telling the truth but it is not in an acceptable form. In the scientific world, as well as in everyday social encounters, it's considered impolite to brag about your achievements. You can brag to your family but in public (writing) you must at least *sound* modest. So even if you've found 'the secret of life' as Watson thought he and Crick had, you express it in a more offhand manner, as in the following sentence, announcing the double-helix structure of the chromosome:

> It has not escaped our notice that the specific pairing we have postulated immediately suggests a possible copying mechanism for the genetic material (Watson & Crick, 1953: 737).

You can appreciate that the authors had to go out of their way to minimize this claim if you are aware of the fact that Watson and Crick later won the Nobel Prize for this discovery. They could have said, as my student would have, '*we have found the copying mechanism for the genetic material.*' Adding elements such as '*it has not escaped our notice*' and '*suggests a possible* copying mechanism' tones down the announcement from a fact, which would sound bombastic, to an idea (*suggests*) which might or might not be true. (I can't decide on the effect of *immediately* as it almost neutralizes *suggests a possible*; it's almost as if Watson and Crick were afraid they might overdo the modesty so much they wouldn't be noticed.)

Words, such as *suggest* or phrases such as *it has not escaped our notice* or longer stretches of text that tone down the strength of the claims are referred to as *hedges*. This word is derived from the thick bushes that are planted around houses in some parts of the world. They 'protect' the house as a verbal hedge protects your claims from coming on too strong. At the beginning of the grief text, the authors declare *In these analyses we **attempted to** identify* rather than *we identified*. In addition to appearing immodest, it is thought that dogmatic claims that leave no room for doubt are not reader-friendly, as in the student's text, *In my opinion, this is the reason for their wrong conclusions.* (*In my opinion* is a hedge although it's overshadowed by the remainder of the sentence.) He would have done better to say *This may be the reason that their conclusions were inconsistent with …* (anything weaker than *wrong*).

How to Hedge

Following are categories of common hedges used in scientific genres. (It is not possible to list all the categories that have been considered to be hedges.)

1. Main verb

   - Smoking *appears/seems/tends to* … cause cancer.

   - *It seems* that smoking causes cancer.

   - Our results *indicate/suggest* that ….

2. Modal (helping) verb

   (For a fuller explanation, see Chapter 3, modals.)

   Possibility
   Stronger: Smoking *may* cause cancer.
   Weaker: Smoking *might* cause cancer.

   Potential (but we don't know how possible it is)
   Stronger: Smoking *can* cause cancer.
   Weaker: Smoking *could* cause cancer (if a certain condition exists).

3. Adjective

   - It is *possible/probable/likely* that smoking ….

4. Adverb

   Can modify the entire sentence:

   - *Evidently/Apparently/Possibly/Perhaps/Probably/In all likelihood* smoking leads to cancer.

5. Noun

   - There is a [strong/slight/remote] *possibility/probability* that smoking ….

   Words such as *supposition/hypothesis/assumption/conjecture* imply that the statement is not a fact but a claim.

6. Conditional sentence

   - Smoking leads to cancer, *if* certain other variables are present.

7. Limiting generalizability

   - Smoking leads to cancer among men who do not exercise.

8. Allowing for human error

- *As far as we could ascertain*, smoking leads to cancer.

- *To our knowledge*, previous research has not done X.

9. Hiding the agent (see Chapter 3, The Passive)

- It is *hypothesized* that ….

- The mechanisms of … *are not clearly understood.*

10. Qualifying

- The X group is *essentially* a population in transition

- We can accomplish this with a *relatively* simple test.

Where to Hedge

Hedges may be needed at any place in a research report but they are obligatory in certain parts of the Discussion section that are based on the author's claims, rather than his facts. Let's go through the role of hedges in each move.

REPORT MAJOR ACHIEVEMENTS (Results)

Results cannot be expressed as uncertain, i.e., *We may have found that* …. You either found something or you did not. However, they can be hedged in one way. Using the past tense (as in b) indicates that the results are limited to the present study. Using the present tense (as in a) indicates that the results represent a phenomenon that is always true.

a. The results demonstrate that women are paid less than men for the same work.

b. The results demonstrate that women were paid less than men for the same work.

COMPARE FINDINGS TO ACCEPTED CRITERIA

When comparing your results to criteria of research, hedging, which I've emphasized below, is recommended:

- Not only did the complicated grief factor **appear** to have content validity, but the results also **indicated** that it was reliable.

When you compare your results to those of prior research, hedging seems customary if announcing better results (a) or weaker results (b)

a. **We believe** the validity of our results is greater than that of prior studies … (Hughes & Hatsukami, 1986).

b. Although these results are **somewhat** contradictory to those of W et al., (Fagot & Leinbach, 1989).

If results are *consistent* with other research, the statement need not be hedged:

c. In sum, the unexpected effects of [x] were consistent with other research …
    (Duclos, et al., 1989).

OFFER INTERPRETATION

Interpretations must always be hedged, i.e., some element must be included to show that an interpretation (conjecture), not a result, (fact) follows, e.g.,

- This result **may be** due to the fact that …

- The results **suggest** that ….

WARD OFF POTENTIAL COUNTERCLAIMS

a. **Raising potential counterclaims:**

A counterclaim that you will accept can be left unhedged: *One limitation of this study* **is** *the fact that* …. A counterclaim that you plan to dismiss should be hedged, to show that you do not accept it as a fact. There are several modes available. You can project criticism to an unknown third party (***One** might suspect that they had better health* …). Alternatively, you can use a modal of uncertainty as in *The exclusion of patients with severe medical illness* … **may have** *removed the subjects most vulnerable to complicated grief reactions*; both examples are from the 'grief' text above.

b. **Responding to the counterclaim:**

The response can be unhedged, especially if it is a reiteration of a result, as in the 'grief' text:

- however, we found that **the subjects who were clinically referred did not differ significantly** from those responding to media or word-of-mouth solicitations with respect to levels of medical illness burden or social support.

or hedged, especially, if it is a claim rather than a fact, as in the following examples:

- Our formulation of criteria for complicated grief differs from past work in that **we think** that specific symptoms will help to distinguish complicated from uncomplicated grief reactions ('grief' text)

- **We are relatively confident** that the differences … cannot be accounted for by a control group that exhibits unusually low levels of psychiatric symptoms (Lehman, Wortman & Williams, 1987).

IMPLICATIONS

Implications can be unhedged (1) or hedged (2), (3), as in the 'grief' text:

1. In future research, investigation of the symptoms and consequences of complicated grief in a less select study group, … is needed.

2. More robust results **might be** obtained with an assessment ....

3. In light of its predictive validity, the diagnosis of complicated grief **may have** practical implications.

Other Lexical/Grammatical Signals

Stating Implications

Implications must carry the following information: <u>The research on [field of inquiry]. is advisable; this research is to be done in the future</u>, e.g.,

- ... future research on these issues will be more successful to the extent that it addresses the social psychological meaning of ... (Shepelak & Alwin, 1986).

- The logical next step in research would be an empirical investigation of the conceptual model ... (Lin & Ensel, 1989).

Although it is not obligatory, a modal of recommendation may also be used, e.g.,

- Future research *should/must/ought to/needs to* focus on X.

Signaling Important Points in Discussion

(or findings in Introductions and Results)

- <u>Above all, /Most of all</u>, smoking was shown to be ....
- Most <u>noteworthy, /striking</u> is ...
- It is <u>important to note</u> that
- Many factors may be involved, <u>chiefly</u>
- <u>The chief</u> outcome, factor
- <u>A significant factor</u> may be ....
- <u>A primary concern</u> is that the participants were volunteers.
- The <u>most substantial</u> issue ...
- <u>Especially relevant</u> is ....
- A <u>key/central</u> feature, issue, etc., is ....

Stating Conclusions

Conclusions to the article can be marked by signals such as: *in conclusion* or *to conclude*; conclusions that are also consequences or the end of a chain of reasoning are marked by: *thus, therefore, hence, consequently*; see Chapter 6 on connectives.

The author may also indicate a conclusion by an expression of conviction, such as: *clearly, it is clear, undoubtedly; [x] cannot be/[x] must be* .... Paradoxically, a marker of conclusion can be hedged, e.g., '*Thus, it seems clear that* ....'

Task: Analyzing Discussions

1. What are the moves in Discussion sections in your target genre? Label the moves in two articles.

2. Which moves are hedged/not hedged? How is hedging done?

Chapter 12

Conference Texts

As a member of the scientific community, you will probably finding yourself attending local and international conferences. Conferences involve some new genres such as:

1. abstracts, which are submitted in advance of the conference

2. oral presentations during the conference

3. posters, which are available to be seen by the conference participants (but may not involve face-to-face talk)

4. plenary sessions

Abstracts are covered in Chapter 13. This chapter will deal with (2) and (3) under the assumption that anyone who is invited to give a plenary session is already an accomplished writer!

Oral Presentations

It may seem strange to have a chapter on oral presentations in a book on writing but talks are almost as relevant to one's career as are written publications. Also, a talk at a conference, seminar, or other meeting, is based on a written document, which follows many of the same guidelines we have been discussing.

There has not been, to my knowledge, any empirical investigation of what makes a successful oral presentation. No one has measured how much material the audience actually remembers afterwards, or what their impressions are. All the advice I'm going to give you is based on my own experience as both speaker and member of the audience, and observations of the reactions of other people. I've tried to keep a record over the years of reasons some talks are insufferable and others are unforgettable (in the positive sense).

There are two aspects to 'good' talks: the content and the delivery. Delivery includes visual elements, as well as non-verbal behavior. The first aspect, which relates to the scientific value of what you say, is beyond the purview of this chapter. On the other hand, by now you've read enough of this book to know that your delivery sometimes influences the value people place on the content.

What You Say—Structuring Your Talk

Although I am basing these guidelines on my own experience, some of them are supported by the classics. As a teacher of rhetoric, Aristotle said (translated from the Greek): Tell them what you are going to say, say it, and then tell them what you said. This seems like sage advice but hardly anyone ever follows it, because they are trying to pack in as much information as possible. If you do this, your audience goes into cognitive overload. Keep references to a minimum; remember you are there to focus on *your* work. Reconcile yourself to the rule that you can spend only about 1/3 of your talk on NEW information; the rest is previewing and summarizing it. This rule will also help you to keep within the time limits. The following is a text I created to illustrate the recommended structure.

1. Give your audience a preview of your talk, e.g.:

   - **First**, I will rapidly examine the structure and some properties of two types of texts, research reports and critiques of research .... **I will then** consider the creation of one type only, namely, *research reports* and **finally**, I plan to consider some exciting recent developments that might link research reports to factors in the human brain.

2. Signal when you reach turning points:

   - Like many other texts, *research reports* represent a combination of two subunits ....

   - Let us now turn towards *critiques of research* ....

3. It's helpful to use internal questions:

   But two questions immediately come to mind. First, how did research reports evolve? Secondly, have they always existed in the present form? One can offer the following answer ....

4. Summarize sub-units:

   What I have just described is the evolution of research reports ....

5. Signal the end:

   Finally, let's turn to some recent and fascinating aspects of research reports, namely, the possible relationship between the production of research reports and the enlargement of the human brain.

6. Summarize the main points of the talk:

   .... In looking at how this field has evolved in the last 25 years, we see that the main breakthroughs has been the analysis of research reports and critiques as genres. This may facilitate our teaching writing to novices. It is even possible that if we understand the structure of texts thoroughly we will arrive at computer programs that can generate intelligent texts.

For connectors that are appropriate in oral discourse, see Chapter 6, Making Connections.

How You Say It

Although conference talks involve a different medium from written papers, there are some points of overlap. For one, the talk must be appropriate to the audience in at least two respects:

a. its level of knowledge

   Before the talk, from attending other talks, and reading the abstracts, you should gain a good sense of what the audience knows and what has to be explained in detail. Are they experts or novices in the field? Do not patronize your audience but make sure you don't leave them confused. During the talk, if you maintain eye contact, you can monitor if the audience is not following you, or is finding your talk beneath their level.

b. its social characteristics

   As I mentioned in Chapter 1, texts must be sensitive to the interpersonal relations between you and your audience. If this is true for written texts, where you (mercifully) are not face-to-face with the audience, it is much truer of a talk given before an audience. If you belong to the same institution, keep in mind your relative positions in the hierarchy. Is the audience composed of your students, peers or 'superiors'? If you are addressing a meeting within a commercial company, is your audience composed of co-workers, managers or top executive level? Can you anticipate if the audience might be sympathetic or hostile to your talk? Remember that any new information is a threat to the status quo. It's possible that you or your topic is controversial. If so, try to weaken the threat by hedging. Do you know your audience personally? If so, you may allow yourself a more informal register.

With any audience, it is well to keep a perspective on your status in the universe. Show a certain degree of modesty about your claims, and refrain from disparaging other people's work. If you should refer to anyone's work, do so in neutral terms. Take into consideration the possibility that some of your 'references' are going to be in the audience.

It is possible to push your own work forward in spite of these constraints; see Chapter 11, Discussions.

No one is going to do a good job the first time. It takes a lot of practice and previous experience to feel confident when you face an audience. I've written an evaluation sheet for talks, which incorporates many of the parameters of a successful talk. Practice your talk in a seminar or in front of a few colleagues. Ask them to rate you along the following dimensions:

1. Was the talk appropriate for the (future) audience?

    Yes 1 _____ 3 _____ 5 No

2. Did the speaker show respect and sensitivity to the audience?

    Yes 1 _____ 3 _____ 5 No

3. Presenting structure to the audience:

    Did the speaker preview the structure? Yes/No

    Did s/he present the structure as previewed? Yes/No

    Did s/he summarize the talk? Yes/No

4. Pace—rate the speaker along the following scale

    Too slow _____ OK _____ too fast

5. Volume

    Too loud _____ OK _____ too soft

6. Did s/he use a variety of tones to emphasize points?

    Varied tone 1 _____ 3 _____ 5 monotone

7. Body language:

    Did s/he maintain an appropriate posture?

    Yes 1 _____ 3 _____ 5 No

    Did s/he maintain eye contact?

    Yes 1 _____ 3 _____ 5 No

8. Fluency (speaking without long pauses):

    Fluent 1 _____ 3 _____ 5 not fluent

9. Dependence upon written text:

    1 _____ 3 _____ 5
    Did not refer to a written text   Referred occasionally   Read aloud from a text

10. Visual aids:

Visual aids were used (Yes/No)

If visual aids were used, were there:

1 _____ 3 _____ 5
Too many   Appropriate number   Too few

Were they easy to read from the back of the room? Yes/No

Were they easy to understand?

Yes 1 _____ 3 _____ 5 No

11. Did the speaker communicate enthusiasm for the subject?

Yes 1 _____ 3 _____ 5 No

12. Did the speaker keep within the time limit? Yes/No

13. Did s/he respond appropriately to questions from the audience?

Yes 1 _____ 3 _____ 5 No (Please explain)

Practical Tips

Verbal and Psychological Aspects

No one can be prepared, like the proverbial Boy Scout, for all emergencies. Just try to prepare mentally for the talk. Try to project honesty and enthusiasm for your project. The rest can be corrected by e-mail. Here are a few tips based on personal experience.

It is difficult to decide what the number 1 'tip' should be. In my opinion, it is: don't read your paper aloud! People will forgive you if you make a mistake in English or if you forget some information. But they will not forgive you if you are boring! I don't know anything as boring as having to listen to someone read a written scientific text aloud. (Try it on a friend.) As I said in Chapter 1, spoken language is very loosely packed, i.e., many words are used to give a little information, while written academic language is densely packed; people who are listening cannot commit all the information to memory. There is also a difference in register. You can certainly be comfortable with a more informal register, while the academic register, spoken, may sound pompous. You may feel that, as a non-native speaker of English, you must lean on a written text. In my experience of 28 years, every student has been able to deliver a paper *without* reading it. Notes, Power Point, and other visuals certainly help as reminders.

Brace yourself for the distractions—people walking in late or leaving early, or conversing with each other while you are talking. If you have ever taught 'adults', you will be used to it. Try to look at the friendly, attentive faces. Don't take yourself too seriously. Remember, people may have more urgent business to attend to. Anyway, you should publish this paper later if it is any good.

Be prepared to cut out parts of your talk even while you are giving it. This is due to the Lewin Time Principle, i.e., the time it takes to deliver a talk increases by the number of people in the audience. For some reason, that 10-minute talk you gave to two colleagues becomes 20 minutes in front of a large audience. Decide beforehand which slides can be dropped or points omitted at the last minute.

Look like you're in control, even if your heart is sinking. If you hit a snag, just pause for a few seconds, take a sip of water, if available. Need I say 'Stay calm'?

Physical Aspects

Have a back up for Power Point Presentations. You may find that your program is not compatible with the computer at the conference, or even that there is no hook up. Just whip out your good old fashioned overhead transparencies. (A while ago, Bill Gates himself made news while presenting a new program at a press conference. The program didn't work correctly.)

Bring a copy of your talk and handouts on a disk (as well as hard copies) and even some photocopies of the handouts. Surprisingly, a photocopy machine or printer is not always available.

Before your talk, try to look at the room in which you will be giving the talk. Check out the technical details such as location of electrical outlets and controls for the screen. Will your visuals be seen from the back of the room or should you make more handouts?

Dress neatly and don't wear anything that will distract attention from your intellectual accomplishments.

Try to stand straight instead of slouching over the lectern. Keep your movements to a minimum. You may need to request someone else to operate the projector or computer if it is far away from you.

Do not stand directly in front of the screen or turn your back to the audience to point to things on the screen. Face your audience and point from the side, with a metal or laser pointer.

Arrange your visuals or notes in a way that will keep them together and in order of presentation.

A Word about Visuals

Visual aids are an important, and expected, component of any conference talk. In fact, they are used more liberally than in a corresponding written paper, due to the lower cost of production. They also help the speaker by accentuating certain points and aid non-English speaking members of the audience by clarifying the spoken points. Visuals, like sentences, should not be heavy with information (taking too much time to read) and there should not be too many of them. Finally, they should be easy to read from the back of the room.

Besides the obvious role of illustrating points in your discussion, visuals can fulfill other functions. Rowley-Jolivet (2002) finds that a humorous picture is sometimes used as an ice-breaker, at the beginning of a talk. More importantly, visuals are used to highlight the structure of a talk, giving the plan of the talk, the objectives of the research, description of the method, and summary of the conclusions. They can be used to illustrate all the signals for structuring your talk, such as identifying subunits, which I've mentioned above. Finally, visuals should not compete with your spoken presentation, but be used in parallel.

PowerPoint

I have lived long enough to see the world before and after PowerPoint. In my opinion, PP has caused a lot of harm to the art of giving talks. For one thing, speakers seem to get carried away with all the gimmicks available—the flying words, various colors, music, and videos. I know that the audience is distracted because often I hear the comment, 'That was an interesting power point presentation' instead of 'That was an interesting talk'. It is also possible that conforming to the templates disrupts natural discourse patterns. For instance, Tufte (2003) has cleverly shown how the stirring words of the Gettysburg address[1] would be transformed into PowerPoint:

On a three colored background, decorated with rectangles, he has written:

Agenda

Met on a battlefield (great)
Dedicate portion of field—fitting!
Unfinished work (great tasks)

But PowerPoint, like the cell phone, is here to stay so I can only advise, 'Use it wisely'. Use black and white and a solid background for text; besides being distracting, colored fonts on a colored background are difficult to see. Don't inject any gimmicks unless they are necessitated by your subject matter. The content of the talk should drive the PowerPoint and not the reverse!

Responding to Comments from the Audience

While they are usually polite, especially in face-to-face situations, scientists are not immune to the urge to show that they are smarter than you. My own research on criticism in written texts shows that scientists can be quite contentious (Lewin, 2005b).

Prepare mentally for the possibility that some people might make unfriendly comments or ask unkind questions. How would you/should you/react to the following responses from the audience, after you have given a talk at an international conference? I've divided them into two categories, below.

Mild Nuisance Value

Someone suggests a better interpretation of your findings.

Someone says your talk wasn't clear about the difference between X and Y.

Someone suggests an improvement on your method such as 'Why didn't you try asking x/using Y method?'

Someone gets you involved in a long discussion, explaining a better way to calculate x.

Someone asks you a question that you can't answer because you don't have enough information.

Someone asks a 'wiseguy' question, i.e., a question to show s/he is smarter than you, e.g., 'Why are you bothering to study X? I don't see where it will get us.'

Serious Criticisms and Accusations

Someone impugns the value of your work, such as, 'Don't you know that Jones et al. (1999) have published results that completely contradict yours?' Or worse yet: 'I have published results ....' Someone describes a serious limitation of your research, e.g., 'You didn't control for social class, as we suggested in our earlier work.'

Someone accuses you of stealing his/her idea.[2]

Discuss these situations with a friend and rehearse your own responses. I can only give general comments—it always pays to count to 10 and be polite. (Aristotle didn't say that; my mother did.) Not everyone has learned this. I am reminded of a student who gave a very good talk in class; when the question period came up, someone asked her to explain a point. The speaker responded angrily, 'I just explained it three times. Weren't you listening?'

Remember that your work isn't perfect and your critic just might be right, even if s/he is showing off. If a question catches you off guard, you can ask the person to repeat it, while you collect your thoughts. If speaker suggests an improvement in your work, you can give him or her credit by saying, 'That's an interesting question.' You can admit you hadn't thought of certain things. You can invite someone to meet with you during the conference, or write to you afterwards, to discuss the question.

If a member of the audience is really insulting or accusing you of stealing his/her work, the main thing to do is neutralize the situation rather than argue. 'Perhaps there is some misunderstanding; can we sit down and talk about it?' Don't sink to the other guy's level. There is an interesting saying: If you wrestle in the mud with a pig, you'll both get dirty but the pig will enjoy it.

Posters

Some people think presenting a poster means putting their abstract on a piece of paper and hanging it on the wall. I actually saw such examples when I looked up 'posters' on Google. The following suggestions are based on reactions of students to various posters and an interview with the graphic artist at our university. Many of the suggestions for 'visual aids', above, apply but even more so, since posters must stand on their own. There will be no accompanying talk to fill in the gaps or draw the audience's attention to important points. Also, not a minor point, people will be standing while they are viewing your poster. This uncomfortable position dictates that they would like to find the main point quickly. Assuming that the content is brilliant, the two most important characteristics of a good poster are attractiveness and readability, that is, drawing people's attention to your poster and then making it easy for them to read and understand it.

Since you will not have a screen to project them on, posters must be easy to read from a distance of two meters. This means a relatively uncluttered surface with large type face (font) and large symbols for your tables and graphs. As in a talk, you must resist the temptation to record everything; a handout can contain the additional information you think is essential (such as copy of the exact questions you used for interviews or bibliography) and has the added advantage of providing the participants with something they can read at leisure later. It also includes your name and address in case they want to contact you later.

The 'portrait' view (i.e., poster is long and narrow) is easier to read than the 'landscape' view while standing.

Design the poster so that it is clear in which direction the poster is to be read, up and down, or across.

Use a variety of font sizes for captions and text, as in a newspaper. Highlight important points such as conclusions. Try to keep equal proportions of text, pictures, and numerical data. In other words, don't overwhelm your posters with figures and graphs, which take time for people to process.

Leave white spaces in margins and in spaces between sections.

On the day of the presentation, stand (or sit) proudly in front of your poster and look as if you are eager to have people stop to look at it. A welcoming smile will do.

As for the structure of the text on a poster, I again suggest studying models from the conference site or from a previous year. For the Population Association of America, for instance, a poster is invited

1. when there is no specific session appropriate for the paper, i.e., the topic isn't covered by the sessions

2. when the paper was appropriate for a particular session but was rejected as a talk

These criteria suggest that there is not a specific content or issue that is more appropriate for a poster than an oral presentation, except insofar as the author chose a topic that is not covered by the conference sessions. These criteria also suggest that the structure of the abstract for a poster and for a talk are similar, except for the inclusion and placement of visuals, as described above.

Notes:

[1] This is what Abraham Lincoln actually said: 'Four score and seven years ago, our fathers brought forth on this continent a new nation, conceived in liberty …. We are met on a great battlefield of that war. We have come to dedicate a portion of that field as a final resting place for those who here gave their lives that that nation might live. It is altogether fitting and proper that we should do this. … It is for us the living rather to be dedicated here to the unfinished work which they who fought here have thus far so nobly advanced' (cited in Tufte, 2003).

[2] For a good example, see Besnard, cited on pp. 97–98.

Chapter 13

Abstracts

Various genres require abstracts. The importance of the abstract cannot be overstated. Although she is referring to journal abstracts in particular, Huff's comments (1999: 67), apply to any abstract:

> I believe the title and abstract of a paper are its anchor points and worth early detailed attention. These two small parts of the paper:
>
> - Attract the "right" audience for your contribution
>
> - Develop their interest in reading the work in its entirety
>
> - Summarize your contribution to the literature in a way that readers—you hope—will remember, whether or not they read on.

Each abstract has its own audience, purpose, and recommended discourse structure (moves). Let's discuss how these factors are reflected in the following types of abstracts:

1. for a journal article

2. for a conference presentation

3. for a grant proposal

4. for a dissertation

(I omit abstracts done by professionals for inclusion in data bases.)

The audience for the first is the readership or a subset of the readership of that journal. Many readers, if not most, read the abstract to decide if they are interested in the article. However, for (2), as Swales and Feak (2000) remind us, and for (3), the primary audience is the committee of gatekeepers (reviewers) and not the general audience; this means the abstract must be more self-promoting than a journal abstract.

In addition, these abstracts must stand on their own, as the readers may have no completed paper to clear up any ambiguity and must judge the paper on the basis of the abstract alone. For your (unpublished) dissertation, of course, the main readership is your committee but they will not depend upon the abstract for their decision; they have to read the entire thesis. Furthermore, each university has its own guidelines for what is expected in an abstract.

The purpose of each type of abstract also varies. The purpose of (2) and (3) is to persuade the gatekeepers that your idea is innovative or otherwise interesting, in fact, Relevant *par excellence*. Although they do not address the issue of the abstract, *per se*, Connor and Mauranen (1999: 48) argue that

> Grant proposals represent persuasive writing. The communicative purpose of a grant proposal is to persuade proposal reviewers and grant agency officials to fund the proposed research .... Grant proposals need to capture the attention of the reader.

These abstracts are written at different stages of your work. Although the abstract appears first, in (1), (3), and (4), you will probably write them last, after your paper is complete and the abstract presents the contents accurately. While (1) and (4) are comfortably written after your work is done, (2) is possibly submitted before you have completed all the work and have results. Possibly, the original conference abstract will not be published as such; if proceedings are published, you may have a chance to change the abstract after it is selected.

Conference Abstracts

As with other genres, it is not possible to generalize across all disciplines, except that all abstracts must be exceedingly brief. You have to follow the guidelines and typical submissions for the conference in your discipline. As an example, I studied abstracts for a conference about to take place at the time this was written and determined the typical moves for the brief (150 word) abstracts that had been submitted for the conference. At the website for the meeting of the Population Association of America, (PAA), I found the following instructions:

1. All authors are asked to submit both a) a short (150 word) abstract to be entered online and b) an extended (2–4 page) abstract or a completed paper ....

   [no instructions as to what should be included in the brief abstract]

2. Extended abstracts must be sufficiently detailed to allow the session organizer to judge the merits of the paper, including a description of the topic to be studied, the theoretical focus, the data and research methods and the *expected* findings [emphasis added] (PAA, 2006a).

This means that the organizers are aware that your paper may not be complete and there is no need to pretend that you have results; see 'When the Research Is Incomplete', below. In contrast, some conferences require that you submit the completed paper with the abstract.

As a comparison, following are instructions to authors submitting articles to *Demography*, the main publication of the same organization, the PAA:

> An abstract of not more than 200 words should appear on a separate page. It should summarize the research and results, and highlight the importance of the findings. It should not include details about the study population or methods (unless the paper's primary contribution is in its use of sources or methodology), nor should it contain lengthy mathematical expressions or complicated notation (PAA, 2006b).

Table 13-1 summarizes the moves of 12 brief abstracts chosen at random from submissions to the PAA conference. As noted above, the instructions do not specify which moves are to be included in the brief abstracts. Following are definitions of moves which were found. As with moves in Introductions, Chapter 7, one move is not necessarily realized in one sentence; it may be realized in one clause or several sentences.

Table 13-1   Structure of 12 Abstracts Submitted to Conference of Population Association of America, 2006

Text #	Relevance	Objective	Correcting/ Gap	Method	Results	Implication
1.	x	x			x	x
2.		x	correcting	x	x	
3.		x		x	x	
4.			gap	x	x	
5.	x	x		x		
6.	x	x		x	x	
7.	x	x		x	x	
8.	x		gap	x		
9.	x			x	x	Metadiscourse only
10.	x		gap	x	x	
11.	x		gap		x	
12.	x			x	x	x

Structure

Objectives

States the specific goal of the paper and names the variables. There is no claim that this objective is important. The objectives can be specified (italicized in [1]) or general, in [2], below.

1. *This study is aimed at* exploring the extent to which religiosity affects the economic logic that rules the relationship between women's work and their fertility (Text 2).

2. This paper examines religious intermarriage across 6 immigrant origin generations (Text 3).

Relevance

Explains why studying a particular phenomenon is important to society or the field. Italics are added.

- Global energy imbalance and related obesity levels are *rapidly increasing* (Text 1).

- Where survey data are used for the analysis of male fertility, data quality *is a concern* (Text 5).

- The question of impact of women['s] salaries on the timing of births and parity progression has gained *a renewed interest* … (Text 6).

- Understanding attitudes toward marriage at older ages *is increasingly important* (Text 7).

- *A large number of studies* have linked living in poverty to poor mental health outcomes (Text 8).

- (third sentence): Nevertheless, the Japanese family system is undergoing *major changes* associated with *increasing* freedom of choice … (Text 9).

- *Considerable stigma and discrimination* is attached to HIV/AIDS in various parts of sub-Saharan Africa … (Text 10).

- *Increasing diversity* has stimulated interest in racial identification (Text 11).

- Addressing *current debates* concerning bidirectional influences between parents and children, this paper … (Text 12).

One abstract includes implications for society, which also makes a case for relevance:

- The challenge to global population community is clear (Text 1).

Filling a Gap or Correcting Current Theory

- Economic theory emphasizes the contradiction between work and fertility that holds in the absence of friendly family policy. We argue that normative forces may offset rational calculations … (Text 2).

- Although sociologists have identified education as a catalyst of social change, the exact mechanisms through which education works are unclear (Text 3).

Findings/Results

In the statements of results below, note:

1. the direction of the relationship is expressed

2. results are given in general rather than statistical terms

3. there are variations in signaling findings (which I have italicized)

4. results are presented in the present simple tense:

    - Three main *conclusions* of the study exist.

        First, religious intermarriage increases with each successive generation …

        Second, logistic regression analysis reveals the persistence of this pattern …

        Third, generational differences in religiosity … underlie the greater religious intermarriage of the 2.5 and third generations … (Text 3).

    - *Results indicate* that educational achievement has positive effects …. The positive effects of achievement are stronger for men …. Proximity to schools increases out-migration …. This relationship is stronger for women (Text 4).

    - *There is indeed a negative impact* of their wages on the timing of births … (Text 6).

When the Research Is Incomplete

1. **Authors can state that results are not complete**

    Preliminary results suggest a significant difference in the impact of education on fertility between religious groups … (Text 2).

2. **Authors can evade question of whether research is complete**

    In this kind of situation, the authors often resort to a promise to provide results. In the following example, it is evident that the authors have not finished their work. Unfortunately, they waste a lot of words with *metadiscourse* (talking about talk) instead of giving information to pique our interest:

    After an introduction, we present a short theoretical background about X, which is followed by the description of our experimental results and discussion. [student text]

    In fact, this abstract could fit any research.

In the next example, the authors use metadiscourse to promise that conclusions will be provided (italics added), without actually stating their results:

Finally, *we discuss these results* in the context of the treatment of family issues in the Japanese media (Text 9).

3. **Authors can state that research has not begun**

… Recent evidence suggests that there can be substantial differences between the population defined as poor according to the Federal poverty measure and the population reporting material hardships. … *We plan* to use measures of mental health at two points in time … to better discern the causal direction of the relationship between income poverty, hardship, and mental health. More specifically, *we will use* fixed-effect models that control for time-invariant unmeasured meterogeneity in the sample (Text 8) [italics added].

An Example

The following abstract exemplifies the moves typical in the abstracts.

Establishing Relevance

Here relevance is established for a current social phenomenon.

Understanding attitudes toward marriage at older ages is increasingly important as young adults delay marriage and large numbers of people return to the marriage market after divorce.

Objectives

This study examines age differences in the desire to marry among singles 18– 69 years old, taking into account selection into marriage.

(General) Method

Using multinomial regressions on data drawn from the General Social Survey (GSS),

Findings

we find that single men and women age 55–69 have less desire to marry than younger singles. This age difference in singles' desire to marry is not explained by demographic characteristics, personal attributes, or marital history. The expected gain from marriage, as measured by education, increases the overall desire to marry, but it too does not account for the age difference in the desire to marry (Text 7).

Table 13-1 shows the wide variation in move structure among the 12 abstracts. Although the majority included *objectives*, *methods*, and *results* (actual or promised), some lacked one or more of these moves. The data collection methods are not always included, possibly when they are conventional or not important, or when presenting the new method is the objective of the paper, coalescing two moves. Results may have been omitted because they were not complete. However, every abstract states its motivation, whether in the form of *relevance* or a *gap*/correction.

Interestingly, nine of the 12 conference abstracts contain a *relevance* statement, usually the first move, similar to the first move in Introductions, as shown in Chapter 7. Relevance is expressed in terms of a social phenomenon or a theoretical problem. The moves use phrases to indicate that the topic is pressing, current, and/or dynamic such as: [X] *is a concern, increasingly important, rapidly increasing*, and of *renewed interest*. This conforms to Swales & Feak's (2000) and common sense advice to 'sell' your conference paper through the abstract; indeed, one of the characteristics of accepted abstracts cited by Swales and Feak (2000) (in the field of writing instruction) was that the topics were of current interest to experienced members of the scientific community. In addition, the problem was clearly defined, addressed in a novel way, and terminology was current, i.e., buzz words were used. (Buzz words are words which are 'in' at the moment; for instance, in my field, we don't talk anymore about students *reading* texts. We say they *negotiate* the text, which may or may not have more of a connotation of getting around the obstacles in reading comprehension.) However, we have no way of knowing whether other research communities use the same criteria for judging abstracts. Needless to say, we can't calculate the weight of a 'hot' topic in contributing to acceptance of the abstract.

Journal Abstracts

However, when we look through the abstracts in a journal on population, (Table 13-2) we see the typical moves are also: *objectives, method*, and *results* but there is only one statement of *relevance*, in spite of the larger word allowance (200 words as against 150 words for conference abstracts).

- The highly masculine sex ratio in India has increased substantially in the twentieth century (Text 20).

  (Results may have been omitted even though the work is complete, because the objective of the paper is to present a new model or new method, for which results will be provided by future applications.)

Table 13-2   Structure of 12 Abstracts from 2000 and 2005 Published in
Demography, the Journal of the Population Association of America

Text #	Relevance	Objective	Correcting/ Gap	Method	Results	Implications/ Conclusions
13.		x			x	
14.			gap	x	x	x
15.		x	gap		x	
16.		x	gap	x	x	
17.		x		x	x	
18.		x		x	x	
19.		x		x	x	
20.	x		gap		x	
21.		x	x	x		Metadiscourse only
22.		x		x		x
23.			gap	x	x	
24.		x			x	x

To see if the abstracts in Demography were representative, I examined one abstract in each of these journals: Am Acad Child Adolesc Psychiatry, Am J Psychiatry, Am J Sociology, J of Social Psychology, Child Development, J of Anthropological Research, J of Language and Social Psychology, J of Personality and Social Psychology, J of Experimental Psychology, and Social Work. The empirical papers in the sample showed a similar pattern of moves to those in Demography, including only one statement of relevance, appropriately from the journal Social Work, which would be expected to focus on current problems:

- Violence against women by their intimate partners remains a leading cause of injury and death to women worldwide (Mills, 1996).

Of the abstracts from these journals, two, from Am Acad Child Adolesc Psychiatry and Am J Psychiatry, actually labeled the moves as: Objectives, Method, Results, and Discussion or Conclusion.

As expected, theoretical papers in this second group followed a different structure from empirical papers. For instance:

1. From J of Anthropological Research

   This article identifies five approaches through which I have attempted to understand the topic of deception and truth .... It traces an intellectual journey through anthropological explanation, tacking back and forth among views that ... [author then lists five views of deception] (Blum, 2005: 289).

2. From *AJS*

Oscar Wilde is considered to be the iconic victim of 19th century English puritanism. Yet the Victorian authorities rarely and only reluctantly enforced homosexuality laws. Moreover, Wilde's sexual predelictions had long been common knowledge in London .... Focusing on the seemingly inconsistent Victorian attitudes towards homosexuality and the dynamics of the Oscar Wilde affair, <u>this article develops a general theory of scandal as the disruptive publicity of transgression.</u> The study of scandal reveals the effects of publicity on norm enforcement and throws into full relief the dramaturgical nature of the public sphere and norm work in society (Adut, 2005: 213).

These two abstracts do not follow the *objectives–method–results* pattern but state the main accomplishment of the paper (underlined). The remainder of the abstract focuses on the background of the theory without actually stating it.

It is not my intention to give a paradigm of an abstract, *per se*. The point of the foregoing analysis was to show the variation in abstracts, firstly, according to purpose—for a conference or for a journal. If the latter, the journal and the type of article (e.g., theoretical or empirical) dictate the moves that will be realized. It is up to you to look for the pattern among abstracts in your discipline.

After you've conformed to the move structure, you can focus on reducing the abstract to the permissible number of words. Chapter 5, Being Concise, should help you in that task. Don't waste words on metadiscourse (talk about talk), e.g., *In this paper, we show many interesting results, and then draw appropriate conclusions.* This sentence represents 13 words with 0 information. On the other hand, if you don't have results yet, metadiscourse allows you to evade the issue. In addition, to save words, two moves can be combined in one sentence, as in Text 7, above:

[Method] Using multinomial regressions on data drawn from the General Social Survey (GSS), [Findings] we find that ....

Language Requirements

Study the abstracts in your target text, (talks or journal articles) and determine the following:

1. What tense is used for each move?

   Are the verbs in the active or passive voice? (See Chapter 3.)

2. If the active is used, how do the authors refer to themselves—*I* or *we* or a third option? (One abstract referred to the authors in the third person: *the authors present …*)

3. Is there any hedging? (See Chapter 11, Discussions.)

4. Do the authors use any evaluative words such as *interesting* or *novel* to promote their paper?

For completed papers, read your abstract and then the paper itself, as a critic might. Do your results show exactly what you stated in the abstract? I have noticed a few abstracts that make invalid generalizations considering the amount of data they are based on, as in:

- Participants tended to choose X

when the actual results showed that fewer than half of the participants chose X.

In summary, your abstract should satisfy two almost contradictory criteria. It has to stand by itself, since many people primarily will consult data bases and read only the abstracts of some papers. At the same time, it should motivate people to consult the rest of the article.

Chapter 14

Writing Professional Letters

Introduction

In your professional life, besides scientific texts, you will have to write many types of letters. The purpose of this chapter is not to offer recommendations for each type. For one thing, I can't offer a generic structure as I have for parts of the journal article. Genres are defined by purpose so that 'letters' as such do not constitute a genre, but a job application letter is one genre and a response to a review is another. Here are some of the types of letters you may have to write in the future:

- Submitting a manuscript to a journal

- Replying to criticism

- Requesting a response to journal submission

- Requesting money

- Responding to someone who has used your ideas without citing you as the source

- Applying for a job or a post-doctoral position

The point of this book is to teach people how to be sensitive to the requirements of the target genre and to model their writing accordingly. Secondly, unlike journal articles, personal letters are not published and so it is difficult to get hold of representative authentic letters. Finally, I don't want to show model letters; there are now books advertised that contain a model letter for every occasion, even for ending a romance. If you use model letters, your recipients will realize that you sent a ready made letter, not a personal one. I predict that they would not feel favorably disposed to respond to your requests.

Letters are also not defined according to the medium in which they are written. A job application letter, for instance, should use formal language, regardless of whether it is sent through e-mail or snail-mail. Perhaps the only difference is that you do not need to include a postal address, as I have done below. It is commonly thought that the rules for good writing can be relaxed (or ignored) when sending e-mail letters. Actually, that may be true when you write to friends or when you write about very trivial matters but not when the message is very important to your career; see, e.g., Gains (1999). Regardless of the content, the external form of business letters is fairly standard, as below:

YOUR ADDRESS or LETTERHEAD

Date

RECIPIENT'S NAME AND TITLE (Try to find the person's title and the exact spelling of his or her name. Also, do not address strangers by their first name. When you write to people in their academic roles, make sure to include their academic title. Both men and women can be addressed as: *Professor, Dr., Dean*. Men and women who are not acting in an academic capacity, such as administrative employees, are addressed as *Mr.* or *Ms.*, respectively.)

RECIPIENT'S ADDRESS

Prof. Joan Distinguished, Director
Center for Language in Education
University of Southampton
SO 9 5NH England

Dear Professor Distinguished: (*Dear* has always struck my non-Anglo students as overly intimate for a stranger, but that's the way we begin a letter in Anglo culture!)

[Body of letter]

[some form of **thank you**, even in a letter of complaint!]

Thank you in advance for your attention.
I appreciate your ….

Sincerely (yours),

SIGNATURE

Beverly A. Lewin, Ph.D. [your name and title]
Senior Lecturer, [position, if relevant]

Encl: [If there are any enclosures]

However, more important than the external form is the content of the letter, which reflects a unique set of circumstances. Although regard for your audience is always important, personal communications—when you are face-to-face with your audience as in conference presentations or when you address a particular person by telephone, fax, e-mail or regular mail—involves great sensitivity to interpersonal issues—such as who you are and who the audience is.

In Introductions and Discussions, the major challenge is to fulfill certain rhetorical purposes, such as *establishing relevance*, while also maintaining respect for your audience. However, in personal communication, social features involved in the relationship between you and your audience play a much larger role, although the rhetorical purpose must also be fulfilled. For instance, the following letters, written by the same person to two different recipients, both accomplish the same purpose—to request a favor.

a. Dear Professor X:

   I was wondering if you would be kind enough to give me your opinion on the enclosed draft ....

   Sincerely,

   James Smith (student in your 101 class)

b. (To Joe)

   Hi!

   Can you help me out? Be a pal and read the enclosed and send me feedback ASAP ....

   Jim

Each letter reflects the difference in audience. Even the openings (Dear Professor X, Hi!) and closings are different, where (a) is signed formally as *James Smith* and (b) is signed with the nickname *Jim*. James (or Jim) has paid attention to two important factors underlying his relationship with each recipient—the social distance between him and the recipient and the relative difference in power between them. Letter (a) is addressed to a professor whom he doesn't know personally; notice that he has to remind the professor who he is (a student in his lecture class). The letter also reflects the fact that the professor is in a more powerful position in the academic hierarchy than Jim. Letter (b) is addressed to a friend, who is on the same level in the power hierarchy (a peer). As mentioned in Chapter 1, these letters reflect a different *register* for each audience.

In Anglo culture, we consider the differences (e.g., between '*I was wondering if you would be kind enough*' and '*Can you help me out?*') as 'politeness' features. In other words, your letter to someone you don't know (that is, with maximal social distance between you both) should be more formal and polite than a letter to a close friend. By the way, the term *politeness* is the way we refer to elements in speech (Brown & Levinson, 1987). It doesn't mean that being polite *is* equated with maintaining distance and formality. A close friend, as in letter (b), might even be offended if you addressed him formally.

A third variable that requires more politeness features is the rank of the imposition (Goffman, 1967). In other words, it takes more delicacy to ask for a big favor than a small one. I've added this variable to our imaginary letter. Notice that as 'James Smith', our letter writer makes a formal apology for the rush, while as 'Jim' he merely acknowledges the lack of time.

c. Dear Professor X:

I was wondering if you would be kind enough to give me your opinion on the following abstract, which I wish to submit to a conference in two weeks. I apologize for not giving more advance notice but I did not realize the deadline was approaching.

Thank you in advance for your trouble.

Sincerely yours,

James Smith (student in your 101 class)

d. Dear Joe:

Hi! Can you help me out? Be a pal and read the enclosed and send me feedback ASAP. I want to submit it to a conference in two weeks. I know it doesn't give you much time but I really need help on this one.

Thanks. Jim

In either case, you might want to mention extenuating circumstances—e.g., illness, which prevented you from giving more notice.

See if you agree with my ranking of the level of imposition in following situations (from low to high).

Requests

- Submitting a manuscript to a journal
- Requesting a response to journal submission
- Requesting travel money
- Applying for a job or a postdoctoral position

Righting a Wrong

- Drawing attention to your own work
- Replying to criticism
- Responding to someone who has used your ideas without citing you as the source

Another variable that affects personal communication is culture. That is, until now, I've spoken about scientists as members of the same *discourse community* (Swales, 1990), which means they share a culture just by virtue of being scientists, regardless of where they were born or where they live now. However, some people contend that membership in communities based on one's ethnic group or language at least slightly influences the way that person uses scientific discourse. (For instance, Golebiowski, [1998] points out contrasts between Polish and English writers.) This is even truer of personal communication; for instance, it has been shown that people from Asian communities show more respect, or deference, to the audience than do westerners (e.g., Kong, 1998). I append the following rejection letter sent to a British author of an economics paper, from a Chinese journal, with the proviso that the authors just *may be* writing a parody of what they think people expect of them.

> We have read your manuscript with boundless delight. If we were to publish your paper it would be impossible for us to publish any work of a lower standard. And, as it is unthinkable that, in a thousand years we shall see its equal, we are, to our regret, compelled to return your divine composition, and beg you a thousand times to overlook our short sight and timidity (Sociologists for Women in Society [SWS] Network, 1982, cited in Izraeli & Jick, 1986: 171).

Sample Letters

As I said, I don't believe in providing model letters, but I would like to show three examples; the first is a general outline of a standard request, which is neutral on the imposition ladder. After all, you are only asking the editor to do his or her job. The second and third letter prove that is possible to respond to a 'wrong' while showing respect for your colleagues.

Submitting a Manuscript to a Journal

Date

Dr. R. Macrae, Editor
Journal of Irreproducible Results
ADDRESS

Dear Dr. Macrae:

(If one author)

Enclosed are three hard copies and one disk copy of a paper entitled,
'_____ ', which I would like to submit to the *Journal of Irreproducible Results*.

(If more than one author)

Enclosed are three hard copies and one disk copy of a paper entitled,
'_____ ', by [names of authors] which we would like to submit
to the *Journal of Irreproducible Results*. Please send all correspondence with
regard to this paper to the following address: XXX (usually the senior author).

(Special problems, questions)

Figure 5 has been prepared in two different layouts so that you can choose the
appropriate form.

(Thanks)

Thank you for your attention.

(Closing)

Sincerely,

Albert A. Einstein, Ph.D.
Professor emeritus
e-mail: _____
Fax: _____

Righting a Wrong

Drawing Attention to Your Own Work

At some time you may find that a review of literature overlooks a significant
contribution to the field—your paper. How does one bring that up discreetly?
The following is an adaptation of a letter to the editor of a newspaper. I have
omitted the identifying details and retained the spirit:

> I read with great interest Professor Martin Lawrence's recent essay on
> Dreams and the Greeks. Prof. Lawrence commented on the lack of
> scholarship on the topic. He might be interested in my book *Dreams
> and the Greeks.* (New York: X press)
>
> [The final paragraph concentrates on the common ground between the
> author and Prof. Lawrence.]
>
> I, too, find the ancient understanding of dreams an exciting subject.
> ... ...
>
> Professor James White

Replying to Criticism

As the writer of a textbook, I am in a dilemma. Should I describe the real world or suggest how to make the world better? It is easy to find instances in which authors respond angrily to criticism, criticize others harshly or accuse others of stealing their ideas. (Refer to Chapter 12, Conference Texts, on responding to comments from the audience.) However, maybe we can affect how scientists act, so I decided to show you instances in which they respond politely. Since I don't have access to private letters, I reproduce published letters to the editor, which of course, might have gone through more filtering than letters not meant for publication. The form differs slightly from the sample letter above.

1. **Criticism about a published article**

   To the Editor:

   We would like to respond to Andrew D. Cohen's article, 'Reformulating Compositions' that appeared in …. While we share his concerns about the difficulties of responding to student writing, we question three assumptions on which his reformulation model is based.

   Assumption 1 ….

   Elizabeth Rorschach [and others]
   [address] (Rorschach, Rakijas, & Benesch, 1984)

2. **Response**

   To the Editor:

   I was quite pleased with the critical response to my article on reformulation. The points that Rorschach [and others] raise are not new to me. I have received these and others from numerous critics. Their statement here is concise and persuasive. Perhaps part of the problem stems from my lack of clarity on these points in my article.

   [Cohen responds to points raised by Rorschach et al., highlighting the criticism not the critics. He then lists common ground in their approaches.]

   In any event, I am delighted that my paper stirred [up] so much opposition. I would like to think this would lead to more awareness … of reformulation.

   [address] (Cohen, 1984)

How would you feel if an author responded to your criticisms in this fashion? If you feel that this response was appropriate, what features make it acceptable? Of course, the criticism was also done politely, making it easier to reply in a similar tone.

Tasks

I've now made a list of a few types of letters you might have to write in your career. As it is much easier to write to people you know, to people on your social level, and to make no demands of them, the list includes only the difficult cases. Assume that the recipient is a stranger to you (maximum social distance) and that he is much higher in the power hierarchy than you, a lowly student. Since we can't cover all cultures, you might compose two letters—one addressed to a member of your culture and one to the editor of an American journal. There are different opinions on how polite Americans are; to be sure, be formal but don't overdo it as the Chinese editor did, above. In addition, Americans do like people to come to the point immediately, as 'I'm writing to inquire about the possibility of spending a post doctoral year in your department'.

Requesting a Response to Journal Submission

You sent the journal a manuscript 6 months ago and have gotten no acknowledgement since then. All letters should start with the reason for the letter, e.g., *I'm writing to inquire about the status of my article, XXX, which was submitted on Aug. 1, 2005*. In the examples below, the authors then explain why this submission is important to them. First, comment on these letters written by students as a class assignment. What are the strong points and the weak points? Let's concentrate on the feelings or attitudes that each student (as author) is displaying. By the way, notice that only two of the four authors remember to close with *thank you*!

> Dear [name of Editor]:
>
> I fully understand that the editorial board [of this journal] deals with a heavy load of submitted research and the outstanding standards of the journal make this procedure long and demanding. However, I have good reason to believe that if this paper is not published in a reasonable time, it will be less attractive due to other similar research that might emerge in this attractive field every day. ... I'd be grateful if you will be able to rush a little this procedure.

> Dear [name of Editor]:
>
> I am aware of the long process of reviewing a manuscript and of the many tasks that face the editors and referees of the journal. Yet, due to the length of time that has already passed, I would like to verify that our manuscript has reached the referees and no problem occurred. I would appreciate it if you could update me about the status of the mss as well as with the due date for acceptance notification.
>
> I thank you for your time and effort.

Dear [name of Editor]:

Our group has published many papers in your journal and usually we received a quick response (within 2 months) so we believe that it is possible that the paper got lost on the way.

We would be grateful if you could check this matter for us …. Early publication of this article is very important since it's in a very competitive field.

Dear [name of Editor]:

Four months ago I sent an article titled XXX. I do not want to sound rude, but we have progressed with our work in the last four months and we have now new results that are also worth publishing. However, we cannot publish these results without the publication of the first article, which was sent to your journal.

Thank you ….

Write an appropriate letter to the editor. With a colleague, discuss which of the following you should or should *not* do in your letter. Add any items you think are needed.

1. remind them that 6 months have elapsed

2. remind them that their stated policy is to give you an answer within three months

3. ask them to check if they have received your article

4. offer 3 new copies

5. tell them why receiving the referees' comments is very important to you

6. add 'I hope to hear from you at your earliest convenience'

7. say that you will send the article to another journal if you don't hear from them soon

8. tell them how long you have worked on the research reported in the article

9. include 'Thank you'

Requesting Travel Money

Your request for money to attend an international conference in Australia has been accepted; however, the Rothschild Fund has awarded you only $100, whereas the estimated expenses for such a trip are $2,000. Write an appropriate letter. Discuss with a colleague which of the items (below) should go into your reply. (We'll assume that your initial application when you applied for the grant did not include this information, except for #4.)

1. express thanks for the $100 award

2. describe the award as 'generous'

3. ask them to reconsider their decision (the amount of money)

4. remind them that the cost of attending the conference is $2,000

5. remind them the tickets are very expensive

6. tell them your financial resources are limited, as you have a wife and child

7. explain why you have to participate in the conference

8. offer to return the $100 as you can't go

9. advise them that unless they grant you the full amount of $2000 you won't be able to attend the conference

Applying for a Postdoctoral Position

The recipient is someone whom the writer does not know personally; since she is a professor and the writer is a student, we should observe maximum social and power distance. What do you think of the following letter? What are its strong points? What elements should be changed or left out? Would you rearrange any elements? Does it sound authentic or as if most of it was copied from the web?

You should mention whether you are applying for a specific position that has been advertised.

If you have a personal connection, mention that immediately, as that may motivate the recipient to read the letter: *We met at X conference ...,* *Prof. Einstein has referred me to you.*

Dear Professor Brown:

Re: applying for a post doctoral position in your group

I am a Ph.D. student at Green University, department of psychology, seven months before graduating in Professor Young's group.

I graduated from Yellow University, in education; thereafter I started my Masters at Green University, specializing in psychology.

I have a multi-disciplinary approach, due to my formal studies and autodidactic spirit. I am a quick learner and with excellent analytical skills, able to work under pressure, process various data into the right conclusions while not compromising accuracy and precision.

During my Master and my Ph.D. I won the T and F awards.

I am a self-motivated team player and leader, throughout my studies, research period and army service.

In the field of cognitive psychology, the leading position of your group is unquestionable. I am looking to strive for the best scientific education. I would like to tie my scientific development with an inspiring research team such as yours.

It will be a great honor if you will decide to accept me as a postdoctoral student in your group.

I attach recommendations, CV, and list of publications. For more information I would be glad to be of assistance.

I thank you in advance for your time and look forward to your reply.

Yours sincerely,

Earnest A. Student

After class discussions, we decided that such letters should contain something to make the professor interested in you and something to show why you're interested in him or her. However, we couldn't agree on the wording. What do you think of the following examples?

Something To Make the Professor Interested in You

You need to motivate a busy person even to read your CV. To say "Attached are recommendations and my CV" might not inspire the professor to open it.

1. During the last four years, I have been studying xxxx under the guidance of Prof. YYYY .... I am a highly motivated, hard-working scientist, and I can work independently and learn new systems by myself. I get along with all people and enjoy the company of co-workers.

2. In my Ph.D. research, I studied [specific subject] and I have a lot of experience with the corresponding WWW system and of course, with the relevant ABC, DEF, and GHI analysis protocols and with the more traditional XYZ method.

3. I am a student of Prof. D. Our group has gained a lot of attention in the last few years since we solved the [X problem] in 2001. I contributed to our group's success by .... My results were published in [name of prominent journal].

4. I am a very enthusiastic and self-motivated student. I have got so far due to my endless curiosity and a lot of hard work and learning. I believe that when it comes to science, the sky is the limit.

Something To Show Why You're Interested in the Professor

You may be tempted to soften your letters to more powerful people with compliments such as: '*Since you are considered to be one of the leading investigators in the field of X*, I would like to inquire about the possibility of joining your department for a postdoctoral period.' However, giving compliments is almost as touchy as giving criticism. As Deborah Tannen (1990) puts it, giving praise makes you sound as if you are in a position to judge someone else's performance. English speakers find too many compliments embarrassing. Instead of '*Since you are considered to be one of the leading investigators ...*' you might just say you found the professor's work *interesting* or *helpful*. Which of the following items would you include in the letter?

1. Don't mention anything about her; she knows she's prominent in the field.

2. I have been very impressed with the work done in your group, in particular _____ and would like very much to partake in this exciting research.

3. I was very impressed by the findings you have presented in the literature. This was basically the motivation for this specific application.

4. I am interested in the field of A and B. In my research, I combined [methods of A and B] and would like to continue in these two fields. I understand that your research group involves both fields and working on new approaches; therefore, I would like to apply for a post doc position in your department.

5. I find your work on gender fascinating and since your group has been leading the research in this field for many years, I would be honored if you could consider accepting me for one year as a post-doctoral student.

6. I have followed your remarkable work of the last five years on xxxx design. I find it amazing that it may be possible in the near future to predict wars. This would be a wonderful advance for humanity.

7. I have been following your group's research for a long time and I really am interested in your research field, as reflected in your website and publications. I am most interested in the recent breakthrough with the xxxx ... and I think that it might open a window for a whole challenging, advanced, and hopefully, fruitful research area.

8. I read your papers in the field and was impressed by the novel methods and creative experiments conducted in your laboratory.

9. My primary interest is XXXX, and, as I understand from the publications on the subject, if there is any expert in this field—it is you. Therefore I will consider it an honor and a privilege to continue my work as a postdoctoral student in your group.

Offer of a Personal Meeting

You might be in a position to suggest a personal meeting. Would you make the following offers, and if so, how would you word them?

1. invite her to the seminar you are going to give:

   Professor D. has mentioned that you will be at our university next month ...

2. offer to visit Professor Brown at her university

Money

Do you think you should discuss the subject of money in the first letter? If not then, when? How would you phrase it? What are the pros and cons of the following approach?

> Should you decide to include me in your team, I will need some financial assistance that would allow me to concentrate solely on my research. I have made some inquiries regarding this issue, and found that $40,000 is the customary fellowship.

Applying for a Job

Ad for a full-time job:

PSYCHOLOGY FACULTY

The Department of ... is seeking Faculty for teaching and research in .... We are particularly interested in the areas of XX and YY. Ph.D. and relevant postdoctoral experience required; successful grantsmanship will be an asset

Applying for a job involves many of the features of applying for a postdoctoral position but remember, jobs are much scarcer. Your letter would have to refer also to your teaching ability and your ability to get grants. What other features might be common to the two situations—applying for a post-doc and applying for a job? What differences would there be?

Criticizing

Perhaps it's not amiss to provide an example of how NOT to criticize. A letter such as the following to the editor of the alumni magazine of the Massachusetts Institute of Technology puts the recipient on the defensive and perhaps makes him an enemy for life:

> Yesterday, I received my very first issue of *Technology Review*. In the very first article I read, I discovered an error. On page 40, the acronym 'URL' is defined as a 'Universal Resource Locator' when in fact the definition is 'Uniform Resource Locator'. I would expect to see a mistake like this in the *Podunk Daily News* but not in a magazine published by MIT. Typos are one thing, but misinformation is a little harder to explain away. It makes a person wonder whether subsequent information can be trusted (Delasko, 1999: 14).

Rewrite this letter, pointing out the same error about URL. Having read this chapter, you now should be able to do it in such a way that the editor thanks you for pointing this out to him.

Responding to Criticism from Reviewers of Your Paper

In this scenario, the editor of the journal has just returned your paper with a comment by one of the referees, who suggests the paper should be accepted, but only with changes she recommends. The referee claims there were significant flaws in your method. You must respond to this criticism in a letter to the editor. The following letter was written by one of my students as an exercise. Although her wording is not the best, Mary comes through as a person willing to take criticism. She has also managed to refute the criticism made by Referee C without making a confrontation. How does she accomplish that?

> Dear [Editor's name]:
>
> I recently received the three reviews, along with your letter, on my paper 'XYZ'. I read them very carefully and found them very knowledgeable and useful for my work and I thank the anonymous reviewers and you. ... Referee C claims that my Methods section has one basic flaw in it—the fact that the participants were not randomized. Actually, I tend to agree with him or her. If the design is not randomized, the internal validity is severely threatened (see Cock & Campbell, 1979). Yet, by examining the results a posteriori one can rule out most of the threats. Cock & Campbell address this issue extensively. I believe that the unique pattern of results obtained in Studies 1 and 2 reflect such a case. I tried to explain this in my discussion section but maybe I didn't articulate it clearly enough. Therefore, I have rewritten that part of my paper and I hope it will now be satisfactory.
>
> Sincerely,
>
> Mary Diaz

Responding to Someone Who Has Used Your Ideas without Citing You as the Source

Let's say you met someone at a conference last year and told her your new idea or theory. You now see that she has published this information in a journal without mentioning that you gave her this idea. Assume she is a professor and you are a doctoral student. Write an appropriate letter reminding her that you are the source of her inspiration. Which of the following elements would you include in your letter? Add additional elements that you think are necessary.

1. remind the professor who you are and where you met

2. mention that you enjoyed the discussion or found it fruitful

3. compliment her on her work

4. mention how you felt when you saw that you were not cited as the source

5. advise her that this is an unethical act

6. suggest how to make up for this act such as publishing a correction in the journal

7. suggest that the act must have been unintentional

8. tell her that she got it all wrong anyway

9. tell her that other people commented on this, since they knew it was your work

10. threaten to take some action if she does not correct this mistake

11. do not include 'thank you'

References

General References

American Psychological Association (2001) *Publication Manual*. Washington, DC: American Psychological Association.

American Sociological Association (1997, 2nd ed.) *Style Guide*. Washington, DC: American Sociological Association.

Bem, D. J. (1987) Writing the empirical journal article. In M. P. Zanna and J. M. Darley (eds.) *The Compleat Academic: A Practical Guide for the Beginning Social Scientist* 171–201. New York: Random House.

Berkenkotter, C. & Huckin, T. (1995) *Genre in Disciplinary Communication*. Hillsdale, NJ: Erlbaum.

Brett, P. (1994) A genre analysis of the results section of sociology articles. *English for Specific Purposes* 13/1: 47–59.

Brown, P. & Levinson, S. C. (1987) *Politeness: Some Universals in Language Usage*. Cambridge: Cambridge University Press.

Connor, U. & Mauranen, A. (1999) Linguistic analysis of grant proposals: European Union research grants. *English for Specific Purposes* 18/1: 47–62.

Dong, Y. R. (1996) Learning how to use citations for knowledge transformation: non-native doctoral students' dissertation writing in science. *Research in the Teaching of English* 30/4: 428–457.

Dubois, B. L. (1980) Literature citation in biomedical sciences. In E. L. Blansitt, Jr. and R. Teschner (eds.) *A Festschrift for Jacob Ornstein: Studies in General and Socio-linguistics*. Rowley, Mass: Newbury House.

Gains, J. (1999) Electronic mail—A new style of communication or just a new medium? *English for Specific Purposes* 18/1: 81–101.

Gibbs, W. (1995, August) Lost science in the third world. *Scientific American* 92–99.

Gilbert, G. (1976) The transformation of research findings into scientific knowledge. *Social Studies of Science* 6: 281–306.

Gilbert, G. & Mulkay, M. (1984) *Opening Pandora's Box: A Sociological Analysis of Scientists' Discourse*. Cambridge: Cambridge University Press.

Goffman, E. (1967) *Interaction Ritual: Essays on Face to Face Behavior.* Garden City, N.Y.: Doubleday.

Golebiowski, Z. (1998) Rhetorical approaches to scientific writing: an English–Polish contrastive study. *Text* 18/1: 67–102.

Huff, A. S. (1999) *Writing for Scholarly Publication.* Thousand Oaks: Sage Publications.

Hyland, K. (1999) Academic attribution: citation and the construction of disciplinary knowledge. *Applied Linguistics* 20/3: 341–367.

Kerlinger, F. N. (1973) *Foundations of Behavioral Research.* New York: Holt, Rinehart and Winston.

Kong, K. (1998) Are simple business request letters really simple? A comparison of Chinese and English business request letters. *Text* 18/1: 103–141.

Lewin, B. A. (2005b) Contentiousness in science: the discourse of critique in two sociology journals. *Text* 25/6: 723–744.

Lewin, B. A., Fine, J. & Young, L. (2001) *Expository Discourse: A Genre-Based Approach to Social Science Research Texts.* London: Continuum.

Lindsay, D. (1994, 8th ed.) *A Guide to Scientific Writing.* Melbourne: Longman Cheshire.

Luey, B. (1997, 3rd ed.) *Handbook for Academic Authors.* Cambridge, UK: Cambridge University Press.

de Montaigne, M. (1580/1943) Of the inconsistency of our actions. In D.M. Frame (Translator), *Selected Essays.* Roslyn, NY: Walter J. Black.

Pechenik, J. A. (1987) *A Short Guide to Writing about Biology.* Toronto: Little, Brown & Co.

Population Association of America (2006a) Call for Papers. Retrieved on 10 Feb. 2006 from http://paa2006.princeton.edu/

Population Association of America (2006b) Preparing manuscripts for Demography. Retrieved on 7 Feb. 2006 from muse.jhu.edu/journals/demography/information/guidelines.html

Roberts, R. Our first globalist? [Book review of *Emerson* by Lawrence Buell]. Retrieved on 10 December 2005 from http://washingtontimes.com/books/20030712-104212-5571r.htm

Rowley-Jolivet, E. (2002) Visual discourse in scientific conference papers: a genre-based study. *English for Specific Purposes* 21/1: 19–40.

Shadish, W. & Fuller, S. (1994) *The Social Psychology of Science*. New York: Guilford Press.

Simkin, M. V. & Roychowdhury, V. P. (2003) *Complex Systems* 14: 269–274.

Strunk, W., Jr. & White, E. B. (1959) *The Elements of Style*. New York: Macmillan.

Swales, J. (1990) *Genre Analysis*. Cambridge: Cambridge University Press.

Swales, J. M. & Feak, C. B. (1994) *Academic Writing for Graduate Students*. Ann Arbor, MI: U. of Michigan Press.

Swales, J. M. & Feak, C. B. (2000) *English in Today's Research World: A Writing Guide*. Ann Arbor, MI: U. of Michigan Press.

Tannen, D. (1990) *You Just Don't Understand: Women and Men in Conversation*. New York: William Morrow.

Thompson, D. (1993) Arguing for experimental 'facts' in science: a study of research article results sections in biochemistry. *Written Communication* 10: 106–128.

Thompson, G. & Ye, Y. (1991) Evaluation of the reporting verbs used in academic papers. *Applied Linguistics* 12: 365–382.

Truss, L. (2003) *Eats, Shoots and Leaves*. London: Profile Books.

Tufte, E. (2003) *The Cognitive Style of PowerPoint*. Cheshire, CT: Graphics Press LLC.

Valle, E. (1997) A scientific community and its texts: a historical discourse study. In B–L Gunnarsson, P. Linell & B. Nordberg (eds.) *The Construction of Professional Discourse*. London: Longman.

Weimar, W. B. (1977) Science as a rhetorical transaction: towards a non-justification conception of science. *Philosophy and Rhetoric* 10: 1–30.

Zanna, M. P. & J. M. Darley (eds.) (1987) *The Compleat Academic: A Practical Guide for the Beginning Social Scientist*. New York: Random House.

Texts Used as Examples

Adut, A. (2005) A theory of scandal: Victorians, homosexuality, and the fall of Oscar Wilde. *American Journal of Sociology* 111/1: 213–48.

Alexander, P. J. (1996) Entropy and popular culture: product diversity in the popular music recording industry. *American Sociological Review* 61 (1): 171–174.

Atkinson, A. B. & Sandmo, A. (1980) Welfare implications of the taxation of savings. *The Economic Journal* 90: 529–549.

Atkinson, A. B. & Stiglitz, J. E. (1976) The design of tax structure: direct versus indirection taxation. *Journal of Public Economics* 6: 55–75.

Ben-David, A. (1996) Therapists' perceptions of multicultural assessment and therapy with immigrant families. *Journal of Family Therapy* 18: 23–41.

Besnard, P. (1995) The study of social taste through first names: comment on Lieberson and Bell. *American Journal of Sociology* 100/5: 1313–1317.

Blum, S. (2005) Five approaches to explaining 'truth' and 'deception' in human communication. *Journal of Anthropological Research* 61: 289–310.

Buiter, W. H. (1988) Death, birth, productivity growth and debt neutrality. *The Economic Journal* 98: 279–293.

Byrd, R. (1988) Positive therapeutic effects of intercessory prayer in a coronary care unit population. *Southern Medical Journal* 81/7: 826–829.

Cohen, A. (1984) A response to Rorschach, Rakijas, & Benesch. [Letter to the editor]. *TESOL Newsletter* 6/84:17.

Colombo, J. & Horowitz, F. (1986) Infants' attentional responses to frequency modulated sweeps. *Child Development* 57: 287–291.

Cooper, V. (1985) Women in popular music: a quantitative analysis of feminine images over time. *Sex roles* 13/9–10: 499–506.

Crowson, H. M., Thoma, S. J. & Hestevold, J. N. (2005) Is political conservatism synonymous with authoritarianism? *The Journal of Social Psychology* 145/5: 571–592.

Davis, M., Lundman, R., Martinez, Jr. R. (1991) Private corporate justice: store police, shoplifters, and civil recovery. *Social Problems* 38: 395–410.

Delasko, J. (1999, Jan./Feb.) Wise king of the web. [Letter to the editor]. *Technology Review,* p. 14.

Dodge, K. A., &. Somberg, D. R. (1987) Hostile attributional biases among aggressive boys are exacerbated under conditions of threats to the self. *Child Development* 58: 213–224.

Duclos, S. E., Laird, J. D., Schneider, E., Sexter, M., Stern, L. & Van Lighten, O. (1989) Emotion-specific effects of facial expressions and postures on emotional experience. *Journal of Personality and Social Psychology* 57: 100–108.

Fagot, B. I. & Leinbach, M. D. (1989) The young child's gender schema: environmental input, internal organization. *Child Development* 60: 663–672.

Fukuyama, F. (1989/90) A reply to my critics. *The National Interest* winter: 21–28.

Gottman, J. & Leveson, R. W. (1992) Marital processes predictive of later dissolution: behavior, physiology and health. *Journal of Personality and Social Psychology* 63: 221–233.

Graves, K. D., Schmidt, J. E., & Andrykowski, M. A., (2005) Writing about September 11, 2001: exploration of emotional intelligence and the social environment. *Journal of Language and Social Psychology* 24/3: 285–299.

Griffin, K. (2005) Sept./Oct. *AARP: The Magazine*: 51–52.

Griffin, M. L., Weiss, R. D., Mirin, S. M. & Lange, U. (1989) A comparison of male and female cocaine abusers. *Archives General Psychiatry* 46: 122–126.

de Groot, A. (1992) Determinants of word translation. *Journal of Experimental Psychology: Learning, Memory and Cognition* 18/5: 1001–1018.

Hakken, D. (2000) Ethical issues in the ethnography of cyberspace. In A. Cantwell, E. Friedlander & M. Tramm (eds.) *Ethics and Anthropology* 170–186. New York Academy of Sciences: New York.

Holmes, J. (1988) Doubt and certainty in ESL textbooks. *Applied Linguistics* 9: 21–44.

Howarth, D. (1997) Complexities of identity/difference: black consciousness ideology in South Africa. *Journal of Political Ideologies* 2/1: 51–78.

Hughes, J. R. & Hatsukami, D. (1986) Signs and symptoms of tobacco withdrawal. *Archives of General Psychiatry* 43: 289–294.

Idler, E. & Kasl, S. (1992) Religion, disability, depression and the timing of death. *American Journal of Sociology* 97: 1052–1079.

Izraeli, D. & Jick, T. (1986) The art of saying no: linking power to culture. *Organization Studies* 7/2: 171–192.

Koester, R. B. & Kormendi, R. C. (1989) Taxation, aggregate activity and economic growth: cross-country evidence on some supply-side hypotheses. *Economic Inquiry* XXVII/3: 367–386.

Lammertyn, J. & Fias, W. (2005) Negative priming with numbers: evidence for a semantic focus. *Quarterly Journal of Experimental Psychology, Section A* 58/7: 1153–1172.

Lehman, D., Wortman, C. & Williams, A. (1987) Long-term effects of losing a spouse or child in a motor vehicle crash. *Journal of Personality and Social Psychology* 52: 218–231.

Liang, H. & Eley, T. C. (2005) A monozygotic twin differences study of nonshared environmental influence on adolescent depressive symptoms. *Child Development* 76/6: 1247–1260.

Lin, N. & Ensel, W. M. (1989) Life stress and health: stressors and resources. *American Sociological Review* 54: 382–399.

Linder, M. & Houghton, J. (1990) Self-employment and the petty bourgeoisie: comment on Steinmetz and Wright. *American Journal of Sociology* 96/3: 727–735.

Mariner I (November 8, 1988) *The Jerusalem Post*.

Miethe, T. D., Stafford, M. C. & Long, J. S. (1987) Social differentiation in criminal victimization: a test of routine activities/lifestyle theories. *American Sociological Review* 52: 184–194.

Mills, L. (1996) Empowering battered women transnationally: the case for postmodern intervention. *Social Work* 41/3: 261–269.

Molidor, C. (1996) Female gang members: a profile of aggression and victimization. *Social Work* 41/3: 251–257.

Novis, C. (2002, July 12) *Jerusalem Post*, City Lights, p. 6.

O'Neil, M, K., Lancee, W. J. & Freeman, S. J. (1985) Sex differences in depressed university students. *Social Psychiatry* 20: 186–190.

Pennebaker, J. W. & King, L. (1999) Linguistic styles: language use as an individual difference. *Journal of Personality and Social Psychology* 72/6: 1296–1312.

Prigerson H.G., Frank E., Kasl S.V., Reynolds C.F. 3rd, Anderson B., Zubenko G.S., Houck P.R., George C.J., & Kupfer D.J. (1995) Complicated grief and bereavement-related depression as distinct disorders: preliminary empirical validation in elderly bereaved spouses. *American Journal of Psychiatry* 152/1: 22–30.

Rabil, Jr., A. (1988) Humanism in the major in the major city states of Quattrocento Italy. In A. Rabil, Jr. (ed.) *Renaissance Humanism: Foundations, Forms and Legacy*. Vol. I: 141–151.

Rawdon, M. (1990, Jan. 15) Flotsam and jetsam. [Letter to the editor]. *Chemical and Engineering News*, p. 76.

Rorschach, E., Rakijas, M., & Benesch, S. (1984) Cohen's 'reformulating comps' prompts questions, [Letter to the editor]. *TESOL Newsletter* 6, p. 17.

Schnake, M. (1986) Vicarious punishment in a work setting. *Journal of Applied Psychology* 71: 343–345.

Schneier, F., Johnson, J., Hornig, C., Leibowitz, M., & Weissman, M. (1992) Social phobia: comorbidity and morbidity in an epidemiologic sample. *Archives of General Psychiatry* 49: 282–288.

Schwartz, B. & Metcalfe, J. (1992) Cue familiarity but not target retrievability enhances feeling-of-knowing judgments. *Journal of Experimental Psychology: Learning, Memory and Cognition* 18: 1074–1083.

Scuglia, S. & Hamburger, H. (n.d.) Dialectic desublimation and constructivist neocapitalist theory. Retrieved on 10 November 2004 from http://www.elsewhere.org/cgi-bin/postmodern/

Sellick, K. J. (1991) Nurses interpersonal behaviours and the development of helping skills. *International Journal of Nursing Studies* 28: 3–11.

Shepelak, N. & Alwin, D. F. (1986) Beliefs about inequality and perceptions of distributive justice. *American Sociological Review* 51: 30–46.

Siegel, J. (2005, August 11) Israeli scientists discover locusts' secrets. *Jerusalem Post* p. 5.

Smoller, J. W. (1991, April) The etiology and treatment of childhood. *Chemtech* [no vol. No.] 207–209.

Song, M. & Ginsburg, H. (1987) The development of informal and formal mathematics thinking in Korean and U.S. children. *Child Development* 58: 1286–1296.

Stigler, J., Lee, S., & Stevenson, H. (1987) Mathematics classrooms in Japan, Taiwan, and the United States. *Child Development* 58: 1272–1285.

Sterne, J. (1999) Television under construction: American television and the problem of distribution, 1926–62. *Media, Culture and Society* 21: 503–530.

Waldstein, M. (2005) The politics of the web: the case of one newsgroup. *Media, Culture and Society* 27/5: 739–763.

Watson, J. D. & Crick, F. H. (1953, April 25) Molecular structure of nucleic acid. *Nature* 171: 737.

Zook, K. B. & Di Vesta, F. J. (1989) Effects of overt controlled verbalization and goal specific search acquisition of procedural knowledge in problem solving. *Journal of Educational Psychology* 81: 220–225.

Texts Analyzed in Chapter 13

Conference Abstracts

All Retrieved on 10 Feb. 2006 from http://paa2006.princeton.edu/

Text 1. Popkin, B. M. The global perspective: an increasing rate of change in obesity and key determinants.

Text 2. Ekert-Jaffe, O. & Stier, H. Normative or economic behavior? Religiosity and women's employment in Israel.

Text 3. Boyd, M., Worts, D., & Haan, M. Blurring the faith? Religious intermarriage across immigrant generations.

Text 4. Williams, N. Education, gender, and migration in rural Nepal.

Text 5. Rendall, M., Admiraal, R., Handcock, M., Joyner, K., Peters, E. & Yang, F. A. Bayesian approach to combining population and survey data for male fertility estimation.

Text 6. Ekert-Jaffe, O. & Mougin, R. The impact of economic variables on the timing of births and parity progression ratio: a question revisited for an individual panel of French women.

Text 7. Mahay, J. & Lewin, A. C. Singing a different tune: attitudes toward marriage at older ages.

Text 8. Heflin, C. & Iceland, J. Poverty, material well-being and mental health.

Text 9. Bumpass, L, Tsuya, N., Choe, M. & Rindfuss, R. R. Changing expectations: increasing happiness and unhappiness in Japanese marriages.

Text 10. Regnerus, M. & Salinas, V. Religious affiliation, ethnicity, and AIDS-related discrimination in sub-Saharan Africa.

Text 11. Oropesa S., Landale, N. S. & Greif, M. From Puerto Rico to pan-ethnic in New York City.

Text 12. Coley, R. L., Votruba-Drzal, E. & Schindler, H. Longitudinal trajectories of youth risk behaviors and family processes: who influences whom?

Journal Abstracts

Demography 42/4 Retrieved on 7 Feb. 2006 from http://proquest.umi.com/pqdlink?retrievegroup=0&index=1&sid=1&srchmode=1&vinst=PROD

Text 13. Ford, K. & Hosgood, V. (2005) AIDS mortality and the mobility of children in Kwazulu Natal, South Africa.

Text 14. Wei-hsin Yu. (2005) Changes in women's post-marital employment in Japan and Taiwan.

Demography 37/4 Retrieved on 7 Feb. 2006 from http://muse.jhu.edu/demo/demography/

Text 15. McCall, L. (2000) Explaining levels of within-group wage inequality U.S. labor markets.

Text 16. Guo, Guang & Harris, K. (2000) The mechanisms mediating the effects of poverty on children's intellectual development.

Text 17. Fong, E. & Shibuya, K. (2000) The spatial separation of the poor in Canadian cities.

Text 18. Davidson, P. & Anderton, D. l. (2000) Demographics of dumping it: a national environmental equity survey and the distribution of hazardous materials handlers.

Text 19. Gutmann, M. P., Haines, M. R., Frisbie, W. P. & Blanchard, K. S. (2000) Inter-ethnic diversity in Hispanic child mortality, 1890–1910.

Text 20. Griffiths, P., Matthews, Z. & Hinde, A. (2000) Understanding the sex ratio in India: a simulation approach.

Text 21. Solis, P., Pullum, S. G. & Frisbie, W. P. (2000) Demographic models of birth outcomes and infant mortality: an alternative measurement approach.

Text 22. Morrison, P. A. (2000) Forecasting enrollments for immigrant entry-port school districts.

Text 23. Murray, J. E. (2000) Marital protection and marital selection: evidence from a historical-prospective sample of American men.

Text 24. Martin, S. P. (2000) Diverging fertility among U.S. women who delay childbearing past age 30.

Bibliography

Genre

Halliday, M. A. K. & Hasan, R. (1985) *Language, Context and Text: Aspects of Language in a Social–Semiotic Perspective*. Victoria: Deakin University Press.

Halliday, M. A. K. (1985) *An Introduction to Functional Grammar*. London: Edward Arnold.

Halliday, M. A. K. (1988) On the language of physical science. In M. Ghadessy (ed.) *Registers of Written English: Situational Factors and Linguistic Features*. London: Pinter.

Martin, J. R. (1992) *English Text: System and Structure*. Amsterdam: John Benjamins.

Hedging and Politeness

Lewin, B. A. (2005a) Hedging: authors' and readers' identification of 'toning down' in scientific texts. *Journal of English for Academic Purposes* 4: 163–178.

Lewin, B. A. (2001) From hedging to heightening: toning down and up in scientific texts. *Melbourne Papers in Linguistics and Applied Linguistics* 1: 17–28.

Lewin, B. A. (1998) Hedging: form and function in scientific research texts. In I. Fortanet, S. Posteguillo, J. C. Palmer, & J. F. Coll (eds.) *Genre Studies in English for Academic Purposes* 89–104. Castello: Publicacions de la Universitat Jaume I.

Myers, G. (1989) The pragmatics of politeness in scientific articles. *Applied Linguistics* 10: 1–32.

Index

Lightning Source UK Ltd.
Milton Keynes UK
24 November 2010

163348UK00001B/28/P